CANCÚN AND THE YUCATÁN

NICK RIDER

Top 10 Cancún and the Yucatán Highlights

The Top 10 of Everything

CONTENTS

Cancún and the Yucatán Area by Area

Streetsmart

Within each Top 10 list in this book, no hierarchy of quality or popularity is implied. All 10 are, in the editor's opinion, of roughly equal merit.
   Throughout this book, floors are referred to in accordance with American usage; i.e., the "first floor" is at ground level.

Front cover and spine The beach at Caracol in Quintana Roo, Yucatán Peninsula
Back cover The spectacular Castillo de Kukulcán, Chichén Itzá
Title page Colorful Mayan calendar, Playa del Carmen

Welcome to
Cancún and
the Yucatán

Stunning Caribbean beaches and epic Mayan sites. Lovely colonial cities and pristine diving reefs. Tropical islands and nature reserves rich with wildlife. Mouthwatering cuisine and vibrant nightlife. Whatever takes your fancy, this region has something for everyone. With Eyewitness Top 10 Cancún and the Yucatán, it's yours to explore.

Set between the Caribbean Sea and the Gulf of Mexico, the Yucatán Peninsula is the country's most popular tourist destination. Its focal point is **Cancún**, a lively mega-resort with a dazzling array of hotels, restaurants, bars, clubs, stores, and activities. South of Cancún, the Mayan Riviera stretches from mellow **Puerto Morelos** and hip **Playa del Carmen** to picture-postcard **Tulum**, with its palm-fringed beach overlooked by a clifftop Mayan temple. Beyond lie the wildlife paradise of **Sian Ka'an** and the diving haven of **Cozumel** island.

Inland are some of the world's finest archaeological sites, notably the dramatic Mayan sites of **Chichén Itzá** and **Uxmal**. The region is also rich in Spanish colonial history: **Mérida** is one of the most delightful cities in Mexico, filled with Moorish-style townhouses, palm-shaded patios, colonnaded squares, and whitewashed churches.

Whether you're visiting for a weekend or a week, our Top 10 guide is tailored to bring together the best of everything the region offers, from the Caribbean hideaway of **Isla Mujeres** to the historic walled town of **Campeche** on the Gulf of Mexico. There are tips throughout, from seeking out what's free to avoiding the crowds, plus six easy-to-follow itineraries designed to tie together a clutch of sights in a short space of time. Add inspiring photography and simple-to-use maps, and you've got the essential pocket-sized travel companion. **Enjoy the book, and enjoy Cancún and the Yucatán.**

Clockwise from top: **Isla Mujeres beach, Cancún's Museo Subacuático de Arte, brightly painted buildings in Campeche, Chichén Itzá's great pyramid, angelfish at the Sian Ka'an Biosphere Reserve, beach at Playa del Carmen, traditional Mexican ceramics at a street stall**

Exploring Cancún and the Yucatán

This diverse region has a fabulous range of attractions, and deciding where to visit and what to do can be a challenge. However long your stay, you'll want to make the most of your time, and these two sightseeing itineraries will help you get the very best out of your visit to Cancún and the Yucatán.

Playa del Carmen's lively and colorful street life is just one of its many attractions.

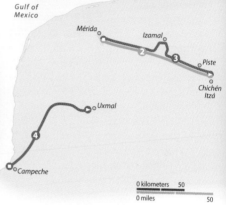

The beach at Tulum is overlooked by the spectacular sites of a great Mayan temple-pyramid.

Two Days in Cancún and the Yucatán

Day ❶
MORNING

Start the day on the beach in **Cancún** (see pp12–13), before paying a visit to the spectacular **Museo Subacuático de Arte** (see p12) or the **Museo Maya** (see p12). Afterwards grab a seafood lunch at **La Habicheula** (see p87).

AFTERNOON

Head down the coast to **Playa del Carmen** (see pp16–17) for a stroll down Quinta Avenida, followed by a visit to the **Xcaret** eco-park (see pp18–19) or a lounge at a beach club such as **Mamita's** (see p86). Or head further south to **Tulum** (see pp22–3), where you can explore the **Mayan sites** (see p91) before having dinner at **Hechizo** (see p99).

Day ❷
MORNING

Set off early to beat the crowds at the Mayan sites of **Chichén Itzá** (see pp28–31), where you can explore the Castillo de Kukulcán, the Great Ball Court and the Temple of the Warriors.

AFTERNOON

Drive to **Mérida** (see pp32–3) and lunch at **El Marlin Azul** (see p115). Spend the rest of the afternoon exploring the historic centre, before taking advantage of the city's free evening entertainment (see p72).

Four Days in Cancún and the Yucatán

Day ❶
MORNING

Start in **Cancún** (see pp12–13) – head to the beach, indulge in some retail

Chichén Itzá, one of the most magnificent Mayan complexes, is dominated by the dramatic stepped pyramid known as the Castillo de Kukulcán.

Key

— Two-day itinerary

— Four-day iinerary

[see pp26–7]. Take a guided tour of its highlights before making your way back to Tulum.

Day ❸
MORNING
Start early for the two-hour drive from either Playa or Tulum to **Chichén Itzá** [see pp28–31]. Have lunch in Piste at **Las Mestizas** [see p107].

AFTERNOON
Head west to **Mérida** [see pp32–3], calling in on the way at the craft workshops of **Izamal** [see p105]. Spend the rest of the day exploring Mérida's historic centre, before dinner at **La Chaya Maya** [see p115].

Day ❹
MORNING
Set off for the evocative Mayan sites of **Uxmal** [see pp34–7] before getting lunch at **Hacienda Uxmal** [see p115], set just opposite the sites.

AFTERNOON
Head to **Campeche** [see pp38–9] – explore the walled old town, stroll along the Malecón at sunset, and then dine at **La Pigua** [see p115].

therapy, look round the **Museo Maya** [see p12], or visit the submerged **Museo Subacuático de Arte** [see p12].

AFTERNOON
After lunch take the ferry over to **Isla Mujeres** [see pp20–21] or fly down to **Cozumel** [see pp14–15] – both islands are excellent for scuba diving.

Day ❷
MORNING
Return by ferry to the mainland, then head south along the coast to **Playa del Carmen** [see pp16–17].

AFTERNOON
After lunch, visit the **Xcaret** eco-park [see pp18–19], before starting your night out at Playa's **Diablito Cha Cha Cha** [see p86]. Alternatively, continue further south to **Tulum** [see pp22–3] where you can visit the **Mayan sites** [see p91]. After lunch, head to the **Sian Ka'an Biosphere Reserve**

The city walls of Campeche hold a preserved colonial Spanish city.

Top 10 Cancún and the Yucatán Highlights

The magnificent Castillo de Kukulcán
pyramid at Chichén Itzá

TOP 10 Cancún and the Yucatán Highlights

The Yucatán Peninsula has an immense variety of attractions. As well as some of the world's best beaches and diving areas, there are charming old Spanish colonial towns, sleepy Mayan villages, and the awe-inspiring remains of ancient civilizations.

1 Cancún
Mexico's biggest resort has miles of white-sand beaches, lavish hotels, every kind of restaurant, and attractions from water parks to giant nightclubs *(see pp12–13)*.

2 Cozumel
The divers' favorite, with over 20 coral reefs to delight first-time snorkelers and experienced divers alike *(see pp14–15)*.

3 Playa del Carmen
The trendiest spot on the Riviera Maya, Playa is on a more small-town scale than Cancún, with superb swimming and snorkeling, and an ever-buzzing nightlife *(see pp16–19)*.

4 Isla Mujeres
This laid-back Caribbean island has a beachcomber style, and is surrounded by superb diving reefs *(see pp20–21)*.

5 Tulum
One of the most spectacular Mayan sites perches on a crag overlooking palm-lined sands and relaxed cabaña hotels *(see pp22–3)*.

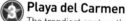

6 Sian Ka'an Biosphere Reserve

This almost uninhabited expanse of lakes, reefs, lagoon, mangroves, and forest is home to jaguars, monkeys, and millions of birds and rare plants (see pp26–7).

7 Chichén Itzá

The most awe-inspiring of all Mayan cities, Chichén has massive pyramids looming over huge plazas, intricately aligned with the movements of the sun and stars (see pp28–31).

8 Mérida

Atmospheric squares, shady patios, whitewashed facades, and characterful markets make this one of the most romantic of all Mexico's historic colonial cities (see pp32–3).

9 Uxmal

The pyramids, palaces, and quadrangles of this dramatic ruined city have a particular elegance and beauty, and are regarded by many as the pinnacle of Mayan architecture (see pp34–7).

10 Campeche

This city is a remarkable survivor from the Spanish colonial era. It includes an old section ringed by ramparts and bastions, and a superb museum of Mayan relics housed in an ancient fortress (see pp38–9).

TOP 10 ⭐ Cancún

Just a dot on the map before 1970, Cancún is now the biggest resort in the Caribbean. Its Hotel Zone occupies a huge, narrow sand spit shaped like a giant "7." Over on the mainland lies the fast-growing town of Ciudad Cancún, also known as Downtown. All along Boulevard Kukulcán are hotels, shopping malls, restaurants, and visitor attractions, including some excellent museums and atmospheric Mayan sites.

The Beach ①

Cancún's greatest glory is made up of fine white silicate sand **(right)** that is soft and somehow always cool despite the warmth of the sun. There are several public access points from Boulevard Kukulcán. The north side of the "7" is best for swimming; the eastern beaches have more crashing waves.

③ Avenida Tulum and Downtown

The hub of the more Mexican part of Ciudad Cancún is tree-lined Avenida Tulum. It's a good spot for a stroll, and its cafés and restaurants are more tranquil than those by the beach.

⑤ Museo Maya

This beautiful museum is dedicated to the ancient Mayan civilization. Right next to the striking modern building that houses it is an archaeological site called San Miguelito with plenty to explore.

② Shopping Areas

Cancún is a shopaholic's heaven, where visitors will find everything from Mexican souvenirs in the markets of Downtown to international fashion in the vast, gleaming malls of the Hotel Zone, such as the exclusive waterside development of La Isla **(above)**.

④ Museo Subacuático de Arte

Over 500 statues **(below)**, created by British sculptor Jason deCaires Taylor, are viewed via a scuba-diving, snorkelling, or glass-bottomed boat trip.

7 El Rey Site

These ruins **(left)** were part of a city that was prominent in the last centuries of Mayan civilization, just before the Spanish Conquest. Close to the site is a re-creation of a Mayan village, giving visitors a feel for the Mayan way of life, including traditional cooking.

A GROWING RESORT

The Dreams hotel at the tip of Punta Cancún is where Cancún started back in 1971, when it opened as the first hotel on the island. The rest of the "7" was then empty except for trees, dunes, and a very few beach houses and fishing lodges. Since then, Cancún has acquired over 32,000 hotel rooms.

9 Laguna Nichupté

The placid lagoon enclosed by Cancún Island offers more tranquility than the ocean, and is a favorite place for water sports. To the west are mangroves and jungle.

6 Wet'n Wild

This water park has slides and rides of all sizes, a snorkeling pool with stingrays and (harmless) sharks, an interactive dolphin pool, and even bungee-jumping *(see p64).*

8 El Meco Site

Near the Isla Mujeres ferry ports, the ruined city of El Meco dates back to AD 300. An impressive pyramid and the remains of an opulent Mayan palace can be seen.

Map of Cancún

NEED TO KNOW

MAP H2 & R2–S2

Tourist Information: kiosks inside Town Hall, (998) 881 9000; www.cancun.travel

El Rey site: 8am–5pm daily; adm $4

El Meco site: 8am–4pm daily; adm $4

Museo Maya: Blvd. Kukulcán; km 16.5; (998)

885 3842; **Open** 9am–6pm Tue–Sun; adm $6

Museo Subacuático de Arte: Blvd. Kukulcán, km 15.3; (998) 848 8312; **Open** 9am–5pm daily; adm varies

■ Buses R-1, R-2, R-15 run from Avenida Tulum to the Hotel Zone (24 hours).

■ Try the restaurants at Mercado 28 (Downtown).

10 Nighttime Cancún

Cancún's nightlife is most concentrated in the "Corazón" but it extends all the way to Ciudad Cancún. A non-stop party atmosphere is maintained in clubs varying from Mexican traditional to modern cool.

TOP 10 ⭐ Cozumel

The island of Cozumel was the first part of the Yucatán to be "discovered" for modern visitors when, in the 1950s, the famous ocean explorer Jacques Cousteau came here. One of the world's largest coral reef systems, Cozumel was declared by Cousteau to be one of the finest diving areas in the world. The offshore reef is full of life and a dazzling array of colors. Onshore, Cozumel has an easygoing atmosphere, ideal for families.

1 Laguna Chankanaab

Created around a natural coral lagoon, this glorious park **(below)** includes a botanical garden, a dolphin pool, a pretty beach, and reefs that are ideal for novice divers.

4 San Miguel

Cozumel's only town has a laid-back street life centered on the waterfront (Malecón) and Plaza Cozumel **(right)**. The island's Punta Langosta cruise terminal is located here (see p96).

2 North Beach Hotel Zone

The island's biggest upscale hotel cluster is situated along a shaded boulevard north of town. Hotels and resorts line a row of intimate beaches. Pools, water sports, and every comfort are on hand, and there are fine views across the channel to the Yucatán mainland from most hotel rooms.

3 Playa Mia and Playa San Francisco

These are two of Cozumel's best beaches, with facilities for banana boat rides, subaqua exploration, and more.

5 Punta Santa Cecilia and Chen Río

The east side of the island is more rugged and windblown than the west, with rocky, empty beaches and crashing surf that can be dangerous to swim in. At Punta Santa Cecilia there's a lonely beach bar, Mezcalito's, which has great views, while Chen Río has a lovely sheltered beach and a seafood restaurant idyllically situated right on the shore.

Map of Cozumel

Punta Molas del Norte
Punta Norte
Isla la Pasión
Playa Bonita
San Miguel de Cozumel
Isla de Cozumel
Punta Chiqueros
Playa El Mirador
Punta Celarain

6 Museo de Cozumel

San Miguel's charming waterfront museum tells the story of Mayan Cozumel, the arrival of the Spaniards, and the pirate era. It has a lovely rooftop café (see p98).

Paraíso Reef (7)

Shallow and close to the shore, this is a favorite reef for snorkeling, scuba courses, and easy diving by day and night. Parrot-fish **(right)** are commonly sighted.

(8) Palancar Reef

The most famous of Cozumel's reefs, with fabulous coral canyons and caves in reds and blues. The waters are full of vibrant creatures, including the luminous angelfish *(see p53)*.

(9) San Gervasio Site

Cozumel's Mayan capital was one of the richest religious and trading cities in pre-Conquest Yucatán. The layout of its pyramids and small palaces gives a strong impression of life in a Mayan community.

(10) Punta Sur Eco Beach Park

A wildly diverse nature reserve **(left)** with turtle-nesting beaches, huge mangroves and lagoons that are home to crocodiles and flamingos, and a snorkeling area. There's also a lighthouse and a tiny Mayan temple.

MAYAN COZUMEL

As a shrine to Ixchel, goddess of fertility, Cozumel was one of the most important places of pilgrimage in the Yucatán in the centuries just before the Spanish Conquest *(see p42)*. A visit here was seen as especially important for childless women, though everyone in Mayan Yucatán tried to make the trip at least once in their lives.

NEED TO KNOW

MAP H3–4 & R5–6

Tourist Information: (987) 869 0212; www. cozumel.travel

Parque Chankanaab: 8am–4pm Mon–Sat; adm $21, discount for under 12s; snorkel hire extra

San Gervasio Site: 8am–4:30pm daily; adm $9; under 10s free

Punta Sur Eco Beach Park: 9am–4pm Mon–Sat; adm $14; under 6s free

Museo de Cozumel: 9am–4pm Mon–Sat; adm $4; under 8s free

Cozumel Parks: (987) 872 0833; www. cozumelparks.com

■ The waters off Cozumel are so clear, and some reefs are so close to the surface, that you can often see as much by snorkeling or free-diving as you can by using scuba equiment.

■ Some of the most atmospheric places to eat on the island are the restaurants scattered along the wild east coast of Cozumel.

TOP 10 ⭐ Playa del Carmen

If you prefer a beachtown atmosphere to the long hotel strip of Cancún, this is the ideal choice on the Mayan Riviera. A tiny fishing village with sand streets in the 1980s, and a backpackers' hangout in the early 1990s, Playa has blossomed into a fun town with an energetic beach scene and nightlife.

1 Quinta Avenida
Stretching north from the town plaza, "Fifth Avenue" is Playa's main drag, for daytime shopping and nighttime promenading – a multi-colored array of shops, cafés, hotels, clubs, and restaurants.

3 Chunzubul Beach
Playa's best snorkeling spots are at the beaches north of Mamita's, beyond the striking cabañas of Mahekal Beach Resort. There are also nudist beaches along this stretch of coast.

5 Town Beach
At the center of the action by day is the main beach (below), with beautiful soft, white Yucatán sand and plenty of shoreline cafés. Beach volleyball is something of a specialty.

2 Playacar
This very smartly landscaped development (below) shows a different side of Playa. It encompasses resort hotels, winding lanes of luxury villas, a fine aviary, Mayan sites, beach clubs, restaurants, and a championship standard golf course (see p62).

4 Canibal Royal and Mamita's Beach Club
Two of the best beach bars in Playa, with chilled restaurant-bars, palapa-sunshades, and loungers, and chairs for hire, plus live music and DJs. Guests at nearby hotels can often use their facilities for free.

Map of Playa del Carmen

CALLE 46
CALLE 38
AVENIDA 38
AVENIDA 30
AVENIDA 26
AVENIDA 10
AVE CONSTITUYENTES
CALLE 12
AVENIDA 25
AVENIDA 15
AVENIDA 5
CALLE 1
Caribbean Sea
PASEO COBA
Playacar
PASEO XAMAN-HA
❸
❹
❶
❽
❺
❾
❿
❷
⑥ 4 miles (6 km)

THE BEACH BAR LEAGUE

Unswervingly popular and the hub of the local scene ever since it first opened in 1984 – when Playa was just a small village surrounded by palm trees – the Blue Parrot *(see p66)* remains the place to party in Playa. Weekly events include foam and glow paint parties – be sure to bring your swimming suit.

8 Nighttime Playa

After dark the Quinta buzzes with crowds strolling, dining, and bar-hopping. With mariachi bands **(above)** in some places and techno DJs in others, there's plenty of variety. The heart of the action is the junction of the Quinta and Calle 12.

9 Xaman-Ha Aviary

The aviary located within Playacar contains a fine collection of toucans, parrots, flamingos, and over 60 other bird species in a lush green setting that seems almost like real jungle. This is a very easy way for visitors to see some of the Yucatán's rarer birds without trekking into the forest.

6 Xcaret

Created around a natural lagoon 4 miles (6 km) south of Playa, this "eco-park" is bursting with flora, fauna, and sea life *(see pp18–19)*.

7 Playa's Hip Hotels

Playa is well known for its stylish small hotels, such as El Faro, and Deseo *(see p86)*. Discreetly spectacular and with lovely pools, they showcase contemporary elegance.

10 Xaman-Ha Mayan Site

Playa shares its ground with the site of a Mayan settlement known as Xaman-Ha **(below)**. Several temples survive, with most scattered around the Playacar area.

NEED TO KNOW

MAP H3 & Q4

Tourist Information: Av 20 and 1ª Sur; (984) 873 0242; **Open** 9am–8:30pm Mon–Fri, 9am–5pm Sat, Sun; www.rivieramaya.com, www.playadelcarmen.com

Xcaret: **MAP G3 & Q4**; 8:30am–9:30pm; tours daily from Cancún and Playa del Mar; adm $100–200; children 5–11 half price (under 5s free); www.xcaret.com

■ Snorkels are expensive to rent or buy in Playa.

■ For good traditional Mexican food at lower prices, eat away from the Quinta. Along Calle 4 there are several very enjoyable, low-key restaurants that serve up bargain seafood, such as the terrace-restaurant Las Brisas *(see p87)*.

🔟 Playa del Carmen: Xcaret

Visitors going snorkeling at La Caleta Cove inlet

1 La Caleta Cove and Blue Lagoon

Both of these are fine places for easy swimming. La Caleta ("the Inlet") was the main harbor of Mayan Polé and is now a favorite snorkeling spot, with coral and tropical fish just below the surface. The Blue Lagoon is a big, ultra-relaxing clearwater pool behind the beach, with islands of thick vegetation to explore.

2 Dolphin Pools

Xcaret has two pools by the beach where visitors can swim with friendly dolphins. It's an extremely popular activity, and only a few people are allowed into the pools each day, so pre-book or try to reserve a slot as soon as you arrive at the park.

Quetzal, Aviary

3 Sea Trek

A fabulous guided walk – not swim – right along the seabed, using simple breathing apparatus and weights to prevent you from floating upwards. You don't need to be a great swimmer to enjoy this, and on the way you see all kinds of wonderful sea life from below.

4 Butterfly Garden

One of the most spectacular parts of Xcaret, the *mariposario* is the largest butterfly garden in the world, partly hidden in a steep ravine beneath a giant net of a roof. Bursting with all kinds of exuberant tropical flowers and plants, the garden is alive with an astonishing variety of colorful butterflies. Mornings are the best time to visit.

5 Aviary and Zoo

Animal attractions are spread all around the park. Among the birds on view – all of which are native to the Yucatán – are toucans, cute aracaris or "little toucans," bright green parrots, and the very rare quetzal, whose spectacular tail feathers were used in Mayan headdresses. Animals here include spider monkeys, bats, and pumas.

6 Turtle Pools

Near La Caleta, you will have the chance to see different kinds of sea turtles – leatherbacks,

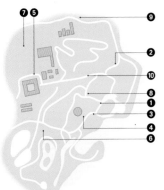

Map of Playa del Carmen: Xcaret

8 Forest Trail and Orchid Greenhouse

A well-signposted trail helps you to explore many other parts of the park, through lush natural forest and passing further attractions, such as beehives, animal enclosures, a mushroom farm, and a wonderful greenhouse with more than 100 magnificent varieties of rare orchid. You can also explore a longer, guided trail on horseback.

Snorkelers in the Underground River

hawksbills, and loggerheads – in every stage of life, from tiny new-borns to grumpy-faced ancients with beautiful shells over 3 ft (1 m) long. The pools are part of a repopulation program to preserve this endangered species, with turtles born here being released into the sea at 15 months.

7 Mayan Village and Ball Court

Reached via a series of atmospheric passageways, the Mayan Village tries to re-create some of the life of the ancient Mayan world. This includes a reconstruction of a Mayan ball court, where a modern interpretation of the mysterious, long-lost ball game *(see p31)* is played each afternoon. There is also a well-presented museum by the park entrance.

Ball court at the Mayan Village

9 Underground Snorkeling River

This clear, winding, turquoise stream allows visitors to swim and snorkel all the way through the park and the Mayan Village to the beach, via rocky canyons, pools, and caverns lit by shafts of daylight.

10 Live Show

Presented nightly, this is a spectacular mix of entertainment spread all around the village and theater. It begins with "ancient Mayan" rituals, mariachis, and vibrant performances of folk music and dances from all over Mexico, and goes on to a *charrería*, or Mexican rodeo.

TOP10 ⭐ Isla Mujeres

Site of the first Spanish landing in Mexico in 1517, the "Island of Women" takes its name from the idols of the goddess Ixchel found here. Though close to Cancún, the island has a quite different, laid-back atmosphere, and has long been a backpackers' favorite. It also has excellent diving and fishing opportunities.

Colorful boats moored at the beachside dock at Isla Mujeres

1 Playa Norte
This beach **(below)** at the northern tip of the town is where many Isla visitors spend their days, with laid-back beach bars such as Buho's *(see p86)* for refreshment breaks. With pure white sand and calm turquoise waters, it's excellent for tranquil swimming.

2 Sleeping Sharks Cave
An underground river meets the sea at this cave, and sharks come to bask, trancelike, in the mixture of fresh and salt water. A must-see for experienced divers – but don't wake those sharks!

3 Isla Town
Isla's only town still has the look of a Caribbean fishing village **(right)**, with narrow, sandy streets and brightly painted wooden houses. There are plenty of cafés and souvenir shops, and few cars.

4 Playa Secreto
To the northeast of Isla town, this "secret" beach is in a sheltered inlet that's even more shallow and placid than Playa Norte.

5 Women's Beading Cooperative
Nearly 60 women are working members of this cooperative and earn a living by making jewelry. Visitors are welcome.

6 Manchones Reef

Isla Mujeres' favorite reef for scuba courses and easy diving. Only about 30–40 ft (10–12 m) deep, the waters are safe and have plenty of colorful coral and fish to discover.

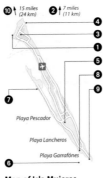

Map of Isla Mujeres

9 Parque Escultórico Punta Sur

The southern tip of the island has been transformed into a sculpture park with striking modern artworks spread around the windblown headland and lighthouse.

10 Isla Contoy

An uninhabited island about 18 miles (29 km) north of Isla Mujeres, Contoy **(right)** is an important seabird reserve for pelicans, cormorants, frigate birds, spoonbills, and others. Day trips are run by companies on Isla.

7 Dolphin Discovery

One of the Riviera's largest interactive dolphin centers, this offers a wide range of options for swimming and diving with these ultra friendly creatures in their natural habitat rather than in a pool. Visitors will also encounter manatees and rays. Other Dolphin Discovery centers are located at Cozumel and Puerto Aventuras.

8 El Garrafón

This nature park and snorkeling center is created around a natural, shallow pool. There are restaurants, equipment rental, and swimming and snorkeling opportunities in the rock pool, offshore reefs, or in the swimming pool.

THE LAFITTES

Isla's most famous residents were the 19th-century Louisiana-born brothers Jean and Pierre Lafitte, considered the last great Caribbean pirates. Sailing south after falling out with the US government, they built a stronghold on the Isla lagoon, but were attacked by the Spanish Navy in 1821. Both badly wounded, they escaped in a boat. Pierre is thought to have died in Dzilam Bravo on the mainland; Jean's fate remains a mystery.

NEED TO KNOW
MAP H2, S1 & L1–2

Tourist Information:
Av Rueda Medina 130, to the left from the ferry quay; (998) 877 0307; **Open** 9am–4pm Mon–Fri; www.isla-mujeres.net

Dolphin Discovery: (998) 193 3350; adm $109–194, booking essential; www.dolphindiscovery.com

Women's Beading Cooperative: 9am–4pm Mon–Sat.

Parque Garrafón: (01) 866 393 5158; 9am–5:30pm daily; adm $85–$199; www.garrafon.com

Parque Escultórico Punta Sur: 10am–6pm daily; adm $6

■ The slow ferry from Puerto Juárez to Isla is the cheapest and nicest ride.

■ Rent a golf cart, scooter, or bike to see the island.

■ Buy food for a picnic at Isla Town before touring the island.

⭐ Tulum

One of the Yucatán's most beautiful places, Tulum offers its visitors a breathtaking combination of spectacular Mayan sites and miles of superb, palm-fringed beaches. Nearby, too, is the finest cave-diving area in the world. This is the most popular destination in the Yucatán for renting cabañas – simple rooms in palm-roofed cabins set right by the beach within earshot of the waves.

① Tulum Site
Mayan Tulum was a walled town and prosperous trading community at the time when the Spaniards arrived in the 1520s. The site **(right)** includes a recognizable main street, the Palace of the Halach Uinic, and the House of the Columns.

② Tulum Pueblo
A rambling place spread out along the main highway, Tulum village was almost 100 percent Mayan, but it now has a bank, bus terminus, cafés, small hotels, and back-packer services.

③ Hippy Heaven
The oldest and simplest cabaña clusters – Hotel & Cabañas Zazil Kin Tulum – are along the stretch of the beach road close to the ruins. Don't come here if you want much privacy or more than basic showers and other facilities.

④ Tankah Natural Park
Part of Tankah Bay, the park offers jeep, zip-line, and canoe rides through lush forests, as well as the opportunity to visit a Mayan village located within the park.

⑤ Secluded Heaven
Along a stretch of beach south of the T-junction in the road is a wide choice of beach cabins, from sand-floor huts to luxurious cabañas, most of them secluded. Few have electricity and are lit only by candles at night.

⑥ Aktun-Ha Cenote
An enjoyable cenote for swimming **(left)**, with a broad, peaceful pool that runs into a dark and mysterious cave system. As you swim, you'll see many shoals of tiny fish.

8 Xel-Ha

This coral inlet **(left)** has been landscaped as a snorkel park, plus forest trail and beach. It has plenty of colorful fish and is a great place for children. Across the highway is a ruined Mayan city.

9 Gran Cenote

Along the road toward Cobá from Tulum are several accessible cenotes in which visitors can take a cooling dip. Surrounded by rock columns and exotic flowers, and leading into into a wide, arching cavern, the Gran Cenote is one of the area's most appealing for swimmers and snorkelers.

CENOTES

Some 65 million years ago an asteroid struck the Yucatán Peninsula, an event that helped to precipitate the extinction of the dinosaurs. The impact also formed vast networks of limestone caves, subterranean rivers, and cenotes, natural sinkholes fed by springs. Swimming or diving in these cenotes, which vary from tiny wells to cathedral-like caverns, is an unforgettable experience. Cave-diving trips are offered across the Tulum area.

10 El Castillo

The most impressive of the Mayan buildings is the great temple-pyramid **(above)**. A flaming beacon lit at the top of the temple was once visible for miles.

Map of Tulum

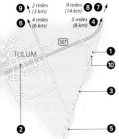

7 Dos Ojos Cenote

This is the entrance to the world's longest known underwater cave system, which stretches over 350 miles (563 km).

NEED TO KNOW

MAP G4 & P6

Tourist Information: www.rivieramaya.com; www.inah.gob.mx

Gran Cenote and Aktun–Ha: 9am–5pm daily; adm $12

Xel-Ha: (998) 251 6560; 8:30am–7pm daily; adm $79; children $40; under 5s free; www.xelha.com

Tulum Site: 8am–5pm daily; adm $5

Tankah Natural Park: 9am–5pm daily; adm $40–50; www.tankah.com.mx

Dos Ojos: charges per activity; www.cenotedosojos.com

■ In peak season the cheaper beach cabañas are often booked up by 10am each day.

■ Diamante-K cabañas, north of the T-junction, have a vegetarian café and juice bar, open to non-residents.

Following pages Carved relief on the Platform of the Eagles and Jaguars at Chichén Itzá

TOP 10 ★ Sian Ka'an Biosphere Reserve

The empty jungle and vast wetlands of Sian Ka'an (Mayan for "where the sky is born") contrast strikingly with the resorts of the Mayan Riviera. Extending south from Tulum around Ascension Bay and encompassing lagoons, reefs, lakes, mangroves, and forests, the area is virtually uninhabited and contains a dazzling variety of animal and plant life.

Muyil Site ①

The ancient Mayan city of Muyil lies just outside the reserve. An ancient city possibly allied to Cobá (see p92), it has an unusual great pyramid **(right)** with a multiroomed building at its top. Beside the site, a path leads to Lake Chunyaxché.

② Boca Paila

Set on a glorious lagoon, the Boca Paila Fishing Lodge is a favorite among serious fishermen. This is also where Sian Ka'an tours switch from vans to boats.

③ Punta Allen

It is said that this sleepy lobster-fishing village, with its sandy streets, big beach, and handful of places to eat and stay, was founded by Blackbeard, whose ship was called *The Allen*.

④ Lake Chunyaxché

Sian Ka'an has many lakes that, like all those in the Yucatán, are fed by underground streams. The channels from the lagoon into the lake have points where the sea and lake waters meet, bringing together a teeming mix of plant life and fish.

⑤ Lake Islands

There are at least 27 Mayan sites within the reserve, many of them small temples sited on islands in the lakes. It is thought that these isolated lake island temples were probably places of pilgrimage, visited in order to perform special rituals.

⑥ Animals

Sian Ka'an is home to every kind of wild cat found in Mexico and Central America, including ocelots and pumas, as well as anteaters, manatees, and tapirs. However, you're most likely to see raccoons, spider monkeys, bush pigs, iguanas, and gray foxes **(left)**.

7 Ascension Bay Bonefishing Flats

These shallows are among the best flyfishing areas in the world, above all for bonefish. Lodges along the road, and Punta Allen's guesthouses, offer trips to them.

Map of the Sian Ka'an Biosphere Reserve

CHECHEN AND CHAKAH

The toxicity of the small chechen tree can make people numb and dizzy by its aroma alone. But if local Maya ever rub against the tree's leaves, they know they have only to look around for a nearby chakah bush to find the natural antidote to the chechen's poison.

9 Native and Migratory Birds

Nearly 350 bird species have been logged as native to the Sian Ka'an Biosphere Reserve, and around a million migratory birds visit each year from North America. Among those easiest for visitors to see are ibises, egrets, orioles, storks, American herons, and flamingos **(right)**.

10 Ben-Ha Cenote

By the warden's lodge at the reserve's entrance, a path leads to a clear, cool cenote, where you can swim among reeds and forest trees.

8 Mangroves and Forest

A mix of salt and fresh water at Sian Ka'an provides the ideal conditions for mangroves **(right)**. Further inland are large expanses of rain forest and grasslands.

NEED TO KNOW

MAP F5–6 ■ Entry to the reserve is $5 per person, but to see the best of the wildlife it is worth joining an eco-friendly tour

Sian Ka'an Tours, Tulum: (984) 871 2202; tours cost from around $90 and above per person (prices vary with tours); www.siankaantours.org

■ The operator listed above sometimes offers specialist tours, such as snorkeling, bird-watching, or looking for crocodiles at night.

■ Tours tend to include refreshments of some kind (drinks and sandwiches usually), but if you are traveling independently, eat or buy food at Punta Allen.

■ Be sure to wear sensible footwear with sturdy soles when visiting the reserve.

TOP 10 ⭐ Chichén Itzá

Built to a scale that seems to be from another world, Chichén, one of the new seven wonders of the world, has some of the largest buildings of the ancient Mayan cities. It had a port near Río Lagartos and grew rich from trading. With a large population, it became the most powerful city in the whole of the Yucatán in the last centuries of the Classic Mayan era (AD 750–900), defeating Cobá, Izamal, and others in war. A visit to these great ruins is not to be missed.

2 Nunnery

The Spaniards thought this group of buildings was a nunnery, but experts now believe it formed the main residential and administrative area for Chichén's lords in the city's first years. The buildings are covered in a wealth of spectacular carvings.

3 Great Ball Court

Built in AD 864, this is the biggest ancient ball court in Mexico (see p31). It has exceptional carvings and remarkably good acoustics.

4 Sound and Light Show

Presented nightly, the show features an imagined history of Chichén Itzá, while the main temples are dramatically lit in changing colors.

1 Observatory

The observatory (above) is also called El Caracol ("snail") because of its odd round shape. Three slots in its top level point due south and toward the setting sun and moon on the spring and fall equinoxes.

5 High Priest's Grave

This pyramid is inscribed with the date of its completion: June 20 842. It is named for a tomb excavated at its foot, which cannot be visited.

6 Castillo de Kukulcán

It is no longer possible to climb this awesome pyramid (below), which encloses an older one, that is accessed from the top of the Castillo. Carvings, panels, levels, and the 365 steps are symbols of the intricate Mayan calendar.

Map of Chichén Itzá

On the spring equinox, the afternoon sun picks out the tails of the serpents lining the Castillo's north stairway and runs down to their heads just before sunset. On the autumn equinox, the reverse effect occurs. This "Descent of Kukulcán" symbolized the city's contact with the gods. Today, crowds flock to see the event.

7 Temple of the Warriors

The squat temple **(above)** opposite the Castillo was used in city rituals. In front of it are ranks of pillars, each intricately carved with portraits of important figures in the Chichén elite.

8 Court of the Thousand Columns

The forest of pillars around a giant quadrangle once supported wood and palm roofs. This was Chichén's main place for doing business: for buying, selling, and voicing disputes.

9 Old Chichén

Chichén Itzá once covered a much wider area than is seen at its monumental core. To the south is Chichén Viejo – a part-excavated site in the woods that is as old as the central plazas.

10 Sacred Cenote

Visited by Mayan pilgrims over centuries, the Sacred Cenote **(above)**, a giant natural sinkhole *(see p23)*, has yielded up jewelry, sculptures, and bones of animals.

NEED TO KNOW
MAP E3

Open 8am–5pm daily; adm $8; free for under 14s; www.chichen itza.inah.gob.mx

Sound and Light Show: 7pm daily in winter, 8pm daily in summer; adm included in main entrance fee, but $2.50 extra for English, Italian, German, or French commentary on headphones; www.inah.gob.mx

■ To see Chichén at its best, stay nearby the night before and get to the site early, before the heat of the day and before the arrival of the large crowds from Cancún at about 11am.

■ The town of Pisté west of the site has several pleasant restaurants along its main street, such as Las Mestizas *(see p107)*, which have more charm than the visitor center at the site itself.

Chichén Itzá: The Carvings

1 Casa Colorada Inscriptions

These record that Chichén lords celebrated a ritual in September 869 to ensure the city's prosperity.

2 Chac-Masks of Las Monjas

The curling snout of the rain-god Chac is depicted repeatedly in rows at the Nunnery.

3 Platform of the Jaguars and Eagles

This small platform may have been used for rituals by the warrior Orders of the Jaguars and Eagles. Its carvings show these animals tearing open human victims to eat their hearts.

Platform of the Jaguars and Eagles

4 Chac Mool and Altar of the Red Jaguar

Reclining Chac Mool figures were fallen warriors delivering offerings to the gods, from food and jewels to the hearts of sacrificial victims. The Chac Mool in the temple of the Castillo lies before a painted stone jaguar throne.

5 Temple of the Jaguars

Carved panels in this temple connect the foundation of Chichén Itzá with First Mother and First Father, the creators of the world.

6 Ball Court Frieze

As defeated ball game players have their heads cut off, seven spurts of blood shoot from their necks and transform into vines and flowers.

Heads of Kukulcán at the Castillo

7 Heads of Kukulcán

The giant feathered serpents at the Castillo probably represented Vision Serpents (see p43) but they have also been associated with the central Mexican serpent-god Quetzalcoatl.

8 Tzompantli

Covered in carved skulls on all four sides, a low platform near the Ball Court was probably used to display the heads of sacrificial victims.

9 Warriors' Columns

A "picture gallery" of the men of Chichén. Most are of warriors in their battle regalia, but there are also some priests and bound captives.

10 Snails, Armadillos, Turtles, and Crabs

Placed between the Chac-heads on the Iglesia ("church") at the Nunnery, these animals represented the four spirits that held up the sky at the cardinal points (north, south, east, west) in Mayan mythology.

Map of Chichén Itzá

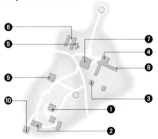

THE BALL GAME

The ancient Mexican ball game can be traced back to before 1500 BC. It features in Mayan myths such as the story of the hero-twins Hunahpu and Xbalanqué, who play the game with the Lords of Death for days and nights, defying the forces of destiny. There were ball courts in all Mayan cities. No one knows exactly how the game was played, but it is thought that there were two main forms. One was played by two or four players on the older, smaller courts, and the aim was to keep the ball from touching the ground and get it past your opponent(s) and out at the end of the court. The other form corresponded to much bigger courts, such as at Chichén Itzá, and was played by teams of seven who scored in big rings on either side of the court. In either style players could not touch the ball with hands or feet, but only with shoulders, chest and hips, so scoring was very hard. Games had great ritual significance, and sometimes, but not always, losing players were sacrificed to the gods.

The Ball Court
Ball courts were found in all the ancient cultures of Mexico and Central America. Though the style and size of the courts varied, they were always I-shaped, as in the Aztec codex illustration below. The game was viewed as symbolic of the cycle of life, and the court represented the world. While games had important religious significance, it is known that men also placed bets on the results.

TOP 10
ANCIENT MAYAN BALL COURTS

1 Monte Albán, Oaxaca
2 Palenque, Chiapas
3 Toniná, Chiapas
4 Uxmal, Yucatán
5 Chichén Itzá, Yucatán
6 Cobá, Quintana Roo
7 Kohunlich, Quintana Roo
8 Calakmul, southern Campeche
9 Tikal, Guatemala
10 Copán, Honduras

A carved stone ring was the hoop through which players had to shoot the ball. It was placed vertically, at 27 ft (8 m) high.

TOP 10 ⭐ Mérida

The most languidly tropical of Mexico's colonial cities, Mérida is a city of whitewashed facades, Moorish-style Spanish houses with deliciously shady, palm-filled patios, tall and plain 17th-century churches, and an unhurried street life. It is also at the center of the Yucatán's distinctive culture, making it the best place to see and shop for traditional crafts and souvenirs.

1 Palacio del Gobernador

Set next to the cathedral, the elegant seat of the Yucatán state government was built in 1892 to replace a Spanish governors' palace. Its patios, open to the public, are decorated with striking murals by Fernando Castro Pacheco, telling the story of the Mayans.

2 Museo Casa Montejo

The astonishing portico (above) of the first Spanish stone house completed in Mérida, in 1549, bears a very graphic celebration of the Conquest.

3 Gran Museo del Mundo Maya

This museum (below) has a fascinating array of exhibits from the Mayan world, and an impressive sound and light show on Fridays and weekends.

4 Cathedral

Built between 1562 and 1598, this is the oldest cathedral on the American mainland (in the entire continent, only Santo Domingo in the Dominican Republic is older). Massive and monumental, it was built in the sober style of the Spanish Renaissance, with a soaring façade and relatively few decorative flourishes.

Mérida

4 miles (7 km) ③

CALLE 43
CALLE 45
CALLE 47
CALLE 49
CALLE 51
CALLE 53
CALLE 55
CALLE 57
CALLE 59
CALLE 61
CALLE 63
CALLE 65
CALLE 67
CALLE 69

NEED TO KNOW

MAP C2

Tourist Information:
Palacio Municipal, Calle 62/61 and 63 Centro; (999) 942 0000; www.merida.gob.mx/turismo

Palacio del Gobernador:
Open 8am–9pm daily

Museo de Antropología:
Palacio Cantón; (999) 923 0557; 8am–5pm Tue–Sun; adm $5; www.inah.gob.mx

Gran Museo del Mundo Maya: Calle 60 Norte, No. 299 E, Unidad Revolución; (999) 341 0435; 8am–5pm Wed–Mon; adm: adults $7; children $1; www.granmuseodel mundomaya.com.mx

■ For some of the best lunches in Mérida, head up to Paseo Montejo away from the main tourist drag. Note that some of the city's upmarket eateries close in the evenings.

THE TRÍOS

Walk around the Plaza Mayor on most evenings and you'll see groups of men in threes, dressed in white shirts and black trousers, and carrying guitars. These are the Yucatán *tríos*, traditional troubadours available for hire to play romantic serenades. They can be hired to entertain at a party or wedding, or you can have them sing there on the square.

9 Parque Santa Lucía

The arcaded square of Santa Lucía, dating in part from 1575, is the most romantic of all Mérida's old squares. Free concerts of traditional music take place here every Thursday.

10 Iglesia de Jesús

The Jesuits built this church **(below)** in 1618, favoring ornamentation and a little flair over the plain style of the Franciscans, who built most of the city's other religious buildings.

5 Plaza Mayor

This spacious square **(above)** was the heart of the Mayan city of Ti'ho, and so was made into the new city's hub by conquistador Francisco Montejo, when he founded Mérida in 1542. It is still surrounded by the city's main public buildings, while its colonnades and benches set under giant laurel trees provide favorite meeting places.

6 Paseo de Montejo

Laid out in the Yucatán's early 1900s boom in the style of Parisian boulevards, Paseo de Montejo is lined with magnificent mansions, some using Mayan iconography.

7 Market

This is the shopping hub of the Yucatán, with stalls piled high with food, hammocks, sandals, Panama hats, and embroidery *(see p113)*.

8 Museo de Antropología

One of Mexico's most important archaeological museums is set in the grandest of all the Paseo Montejo mansions, built for General Francisco Cantón between 1909 and 1911. It has many treasures excavated from sites across the Yucatán, and is especially rich in ceramics and jade. It offers an overview of the Mayan world that illuminates visits to the site.

TOP 10 ⭐ Uxmal

The most majestic of the ruined Mayan cities, Uxmal (which means "three-times-built") was a powerful city state from AD 700 to 900. Its spectacular buildings resemble gigantic stage sets and have been compared to the famous monuments of Greece and Rome.

Pyramid of the Magician ①

Unusually, Uxmal's best-known pyramid (right) has rounded corners. The temple at the top is the legendary home of the Dwarf of Uxmal. Sadly, visitors can no longer climb to the top.

② House of the Pigeons

This splendid complex consists of temples and palatial residences, once covered in sculptures. Early travelers thought the lofty roof comb above its central quadrangle looked like dovecotes (below), hence the name.

③ Temple of the Centipede and the Arch

Unexcavated areas include the Temple of the Centipede. The sacbé (Mayan road) leading to it continued to the allied city of Kabah. An arch marks the boundary of Uxmal's central core.

Map of Uxmal

④ Great Pyramid

Many parts of this towering pyramid are older than the Governor's Palace next door. Like many Mayan buildings, it was altered and added to many times but is now in poor condition.

5 House of the Old Woman

Only partly excavated, this large pyramid with a Puuc-style temple on one side is among the oldest major structures at Uxmal, dating from about AD 700. In Mayan legend, it is said to be the home of the Sprite's Mother.

6 Sound and Light Show

Every night, Uxmal's major buildings are dramatically lit up in varying colors **(above)**, and there is a commentary on Uxmal in history and legend.

7 Nunnery Quadrangle

This elegant complex of four buildings was at the heart of Uxmal's power and ritual. It was so named by a Spanish friar merely because its structure reminded him of a convent. Its façade's intricate carvings *(see p36)* symbolize the magical authority of the city and its rulers and their contact with the gods.

8 House of the Turtles

This small, delicately proportioned temple-residence is considered the archetype of the pure Puuc architectural style *(see p37)*. The name comes from its decorative cornice, featuring a line of turtles carved in stone. This is a motif that is seen many times at Uxmal; it was associated with the rebirth of new life and the fertility of the coming of the rains.

UXMAL'S SPRITE

In Mayan legend, Uxmal was founded by an *alux* (sprite), who had defied the authority of a local king. When the king dared the sprite to build a house, the Pyramid of the Magician appeared overnight. On another day the sprite built the path to Kabah. The king's last test was that they should both be hit on the head with hammers. The king died, but the sprite was protected by a magic tortilla and went on to rule Uxmal.

9 Ball Court

Uxmal's main Ball Court is smaller than the Great Court at Chichén Itzá *(see p31)*. The original scoring rings are inscribed with dates from the year 901; those you see at the court are replicas **(above)**.

10 Governor's Palace

Often regarded as the finest of all Mayan buildings, this huge palace, over 300 ft (91 m) long, was built for the greatest of Uxmal's rulers, known as Chan-Chak-Kaknal-Ahaw, or Lord Chak. Its huge frieze symbolizes the passage of time as well as the cycles of rain, sun, and rebirth.

NEED TO KNOW

MAP C4

Open 8am–5pm daily; adm $15 Mon–Sat, give a tip for the guided visit; www.inah.gob.mx

Sound and Light Show: 7pm daily in winter, 8pm daily in summer; adm $8

■ Arrive at the site early to miss the heat and the crowds. Allow at least a full morning to explore the whole site.

■ Hal-Tun, set beside the road about a mile (2 km) north of the site, is a charming traditional Yucatecan restaurant with an airy, relaxing terrace.

Uxmal: The Carvings

1 Monstermouths

Temple entrances in the form of giant monster-like faces, such as on the House of the Dwarf at the Pyramid of the Magician, made a striking connection between the temple and the gods of the earth.

2 Nunnery: Vision Serpents

The patterns on the East Building are Vision Serpents, conduits between men and the "Otherworld."

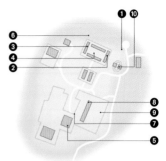

Map of Uxmal's Carvings

Serpent heads at the Nunnery

3 Nunnery: Serpent Heads

The huge feathered snakes winding around the West Building are probably Vision Serpents. Human faces emerge from their jaws.

4 Nunnery Quadrangle: Mayan Huts

A distinctive feature of Puuc carving is the combination of complex symbols with everyday images. The huts carved on the South Building of the Nunnery are very little different from those seen in Yucatecan villages today.

5 Parrots of the Great Pyramid

Stylized *guaca-mayas* (macaws) feature prominently as symbols of uncontrolled nature in the carvings on the temple at the top of the ruined Great Pyramid.

6 Nunnery: Flowers and Lattices

Lattice work represented the huts in which meetings were held, while flowers symbolized magic. The combination of the two denoted a ceremonial site.

7 Muyal Symbols

The simple spiral pattern seen frequently on the Nunnery and Governor's Palace represents the Mayan word for cloud, *muyal*, yet another symbol of contact with the heavens.

8 Lord Chak

The figure in a spectacular headdress set within the façade of the Governor's Palace is believed to be Lord Chak himself.

9 La Picota

The phallic column called the "whipping-post" in Spanish has inscriptions on it that have never been deciphered. It formed part of a fertility cult that was a distinctive feature of Uxmal.

Parrot carving at the Birds Quadrangle

10 Birds Quadrangle

The beautiful images of parrots and other birds carved here symbolized the unpredictable elements in nature.

THE PUUC CITIES

Uxmal was the largest of a string of Mayan communities that flourished in the Puuc Hills of southern Yucatán around AD 650–920. The other well-known cities are Kabah, Sayil, Xlapak, and Labná *(see pp44–5)*. Their very distinctive style of architecture is the most refined of those used by Mayan builders, and is characterized by strong horizontal lines, elegant proportions, and a sharp contrast between very plain lower walls and rows of elaborately carved friezes above them. Many architectural details seem to mimic humbler buildings and natural features, such as the small drum columns along the bottom of many Puuc walls, which imitate the stick walls of village huts. The communities that lived in these cities were wealthy but fragile, because this region is one of the driest parts of the Yucatán. Indeed, severe drought was probably a major reason why the southern Mayan cities collapsed very quickly, in AD 800–950 *(see p42)*. A one- or two-day tour of the main Puuc cities is possible, following the recognized Puuc Route, south of Uxmal.

Mayan Puuc-style carving can clearly be seen here on the grand Arch of Labná *(see p109)*.

Kabah's Codz Poop
The main façade of the Codz Poop (Palace of Masks) at Kabah is covered in over 250 faces of the rain-god Chac *(see p43)*. The Maya believed that covering structures with images of gods gave the buildings divine powers.

⭐ Campeche

The Old City of Campeche is a remarkable museum piece of the colonial era. Cobbled streets of aged houses painted in delicate blues, greens, and ochers still sit within the city walls, which were built to fend off pirate attacks when this was one of the great trading strongholds of the Spanish empire. Campeche's actual museum, housed in an old fortress, displays spectacular Mayan relics from the excavated forest city of Calakmul.

1 Palacio Centro Cultural

Housed in an attractive colonial-era building on the Parque Principal, this museum innovatively charts the history of the city through multimedia displays, a sound and light show, and exhibits that include a replica Spanish galleon.

4 Casa Seis

A gracious old house on the west side of the Parque Principal, this has been restored to re-create the home of a prosperous 19th-century Campeche merchant. The house's patio hosts a tourist information desk and also features concerts and exhibitions.

2 Fuerte San Miguel Museum

A hilltop fortress **(above)** just south of the city, this is now home to a fine collection of Mayan relics, including a set of beautiful jade funeral masks.

5 The Malecón

This waterfront has been attractively restored and is a popular place for locals to take an evening stroll. There are often superb sunsets over the Gulf of Mexico.

7 Puerta de Tierra

Built in 1732, the Puerta de Tierra ("Land Gate") was the only way in or out of Campeche on the landward side. Within is a museum of maritime and pirate history.

3 Puerta de Mar

After the city walls were built, Puerta de Mar provided the only gateway to the harbor. The bastion now houses the Museo de las Estelas Mayas, displaying Mayan carvings from sites around Campeche.

6 Cathedral

Begun in the 1560s, the cathedral in Campeche **(right)** was not completed until the 19th century. Its façade is one of the oldest parts, designed in a Spanish Renaissance style typical of many churches built in the reign of King Philip II.

Gulf of Mexico

Map of Campeche

❶
❸
❺
❷ 3 miles (5 km)
❽
❾ 2 miles (3 km)
AV. MIGUEL ALEMAN
CALLE 12
CALLE 8
AV. RUIZ CORTINES
CALLE 10
CALLE 12
CALLE 14
CALLE 16
CALLE 18
CALLE 67
CALLE 65
CALLE 63
CALLE 53
CALLE 55
CIRCUITO BALUARTES
AV. GOBERNADORES
C. TALAMANTES
CIRCUITO BALUARTES
❻
❹
❿
❼ 30 miles (50 km)

THE PIRATE PLAGUE

Between the 1560s and the 1680s Campeche was attacked again and again by pirates such as Henry Morgan and the Dutchman known only as "Peg-Leg." Finally, the Spanish governors and city's merchants had suffered enough and ordered the building of a solid ring of walls and bastions. Campeche was transformed into one of the largest walled cities in Spanish America.

Street in Campeche's colonial Old City

⑧ Baluarte de Santiago

This isolated bastion has been imaginatively used to house a dense and verdant botanical garden, with giant palms and other lush tropical flora.

⑨ Fuerte San José Museum

This sturdy Spanish fortress houses the Post-Conquest sections of the town's museum. There are lovely sea and city views from the ramparts.

⑩ Edzná

The city of Edzná, 30 miles (48 km) southeast of Campeche, once rivalled Chichén Itzá and Uxmal in size and wealth. Its palace-temple, known as the "Building of the Five Stories" **(above)**, is one of the largest, most intricate Mayan buildings.

NEED TO KNOW

MAP A5

Tourist Information:
Casa Seis, Av Ruiz Cortines; (981) 127 3300

Palacio Centro Cultural: Calle 8, between 55–7; (981) 811 0366; 10am–7pm Tue–Sun

Museo de las Estelas Mayas: 8am–5pm Tue–Sun

Puerta de Tierra: 9am–8pm

Fuerte San Miguel: 8:30am–5pm Tue–Sun; adm $2.50

Fuerte San José: 9:30am–5:30pm Tue–Sun; adm $3

Edzná: 8am–5pm Mon–Sun; adm $3; www.inah. gob.mx

■ "El Guapo" buses run to the fortress museums from the Parque Principal.

■ Cheerful Luz de Luna (Calle 59, No. 6) offers a range of good-value Mexican dishes.

The Top 10
of Everything

Dancers at the Mérida en Domingo weekly fiesta

🔟 Moments in History

1 2000 BC–AD 100: Early Cultures

The Maya emerged in the Yucatán perhaps as early as 2000 BC. But it is not until 300 BC–AD 100 that the distinctive characteristics of their culture appeared – such as a writing system, calendar, and city states. For these attributes, the Maya owe much to the first great culture of ancient Mexico, the Olmecs, who thrived between 1500 and 300 BC.

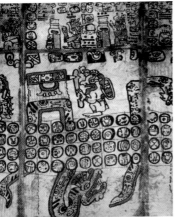

Mayan codices, Museo Maya, Cancún

2 250–800: Classic Era Mayan Civilization

For over 500 years in the Classic era, Mayan civilization flourished throughout the Yucatán, Chiapas, northern Guatemala, and Belize. And, from about 650, the culture expanded vigorously in the northern Yucatán, reaching its peak at Chichén Itzá and Uxmal.

3 800–950: Collapse of Mayan Civilization

In the relatively short span of about 150 years, Mayan civilization almost disappeared, most likely due to a series of catastrophes – over-population, over-use of exhausted land, intensification of inter-Mayan wars, and drought. The southern city states were left deserted, and the Mayan writing system virtually disappeared. In the north, the decline occurred later, and the cities were never entirely abandoned.

4 1150–1520: Post-classic Revival of Mayan Culture

After a 200-year gap, Mayan culture was revived on a modest scale in the northern Yucatán, with the city of Mayapán. Smaller cities, such as Cozumel, El Rey (Cancún), and Tulum developed near the Yucatán coast and became important links in a trade route between the Aztecs of Central Mexico and South America.

5 1517: Spaniards Arrive

An expedition led by Francisco Hernández de Córdoba sailed from Cuba and made the first Spanish landfall in Mexico, on Isla Mujeres. It continued to Campeche and Champotón, but it was then attacked by the Maya and forced to turn back.

6 1526–42: Spanish Conquest of the Yucatán

The Yucatán was conquered on the third attempt by conquistadores led by three members of the Montejo family. Having been besieged for months in the ruins of ancient Ti'ho, they made it the site of their new city of Mérida.

Painting depicting the conquistadors

Yucatán Independence ceremony

7 1821: Independence

As Spain's American Empire collapsed, the Yucatán, which had had its own administration under Spanish rule, grudgingly agreed to become part of an independent Mexico, but declared independence a few years later. In 1842 a Mexican attempt to reincorporate the Yucatán by force was beaten back.

8 1847: Caste War Begins

Mayans across the Yucatán rose against their white and *mestizo* (mixed-race) rulers in the best-organized Native American revolt anywhere in the Americas since the Conquest – and almost succeeded. The main Caste War was over by 1850, but rebels continued to defy Mexico until 1902 – some until 1930.

9 1860–1910: Henequén Boom

Global demand soared for sisal rope, made from the *henequén* agave, transforming the Yucatán's economy. This "green gold" was the world's best rope until the synthetics of the 1950s. New wealth was reflected in Mérida's extravagant mansions, theaters, and other attractions for *henequén* magnates. The boom even partly survived the Mexican Revolution, which began in 1910.

10 1971: Tourism Arrives

Cancún's first hotel opened and another economic transformation began with the dawn of tourism.

TOP 10 GODS AND SPIRITS OF THE ANCIENT MAYA

1 Itzamná
Paramount god in the Post-classic Yucatán, he is the god of medicine and the inventor of writing.

2 Ixchel
The goddess of fertility, childbirth, and weaving.

3 Maize God
One of the foremost gods, created by the First Mother and First Father (maize was essential in ancient America).

4 Hero Twins
In Mayan myths, the twins Hunahpú and Xbalanqué have many adventures and defy the forces of death.

5 Chac
The Mayan god of rain and lightning, he is identifiable in carvings by his long, curling snout.

6 Tlaloc
A Central Mexican god of rain and war, with strange "goggles" on his eyes.

7 Kukulcán
A powerful bird-serpent, the Central Mexican god Quetzalcoatl was known in the Yucatán as Kukulcán.

8 Vision Serpents
Conduits between men and the gods, they were summoned up by Mayan lords and shamans during rituals.

9 Cosmic Turtle
Another symbol of water and the earth. In the Mayan creation myth, the Maize God emerges through a crack in the shell of the cosmic turtle.

10 Earth Lord
The Maya viewed the earth as a living being, which could be either kindly or monstrous. Monstermouth temples (*see p36*) are often representations of the Earth Lord.

Chac, the god of rain

🔟 Popular Mayan Sites

① Labná

MAP C4

One of the most beautiful Mayan sites, this is set in a wooded valley full of colorful birds and retains a strong impression of the life that went on here. It boasts fine buildings, above all the Arch of Labná *(see p109)*.

Doorway in a Labná building

② Kabah

MAP C4

This is second in importance among the Puuc cities *(see p37)* after Uxmal, to which it was linked by a *sacbé* or Mayan road. A grand arch over the end of this path forms a pair with the arch at Uxmal *(see pp34–7)*. The great highlight is the Codz-Poop or "Palace of Masks," with a façade that has over 250 long-nosed Chac faces *(see p110)*.

Buildings in the Kabah complex

③ Ek-Balam

MAP F2

This compact city was little known, but excavations of its largest temple-mound in 1998 revealed spectacular carvings, especially at El Trono ("The Throne"), the largest and most extravagant of Mayan monster-mouth temples. Other unique buildings include an almost spiral-shaped tower, La Redonda, the design of which is a mystery *(see p102)*.

④ Sayil

MAP C4

With around 17,000 inhabitants in AD 850, Sayil was among the wealthiest of the Puuc towns. Its magnificent Palacio has been likened to ancient Greek buildings. The Mirador pyramid was the center of the town's market area *(see p110)*.

⑤ Dzibilchaltún

MAP C2

Located just north of Mérida, this site was occupied for over 2,000 years. At dawn on spring and summer equinoxes, the sun strikes straight through the open doorways of the Temple of the Seven Dolls and along a road. There's also a great swimming cenote located here *(see p59 and 110)*.

⑥ Chichén Itzá

MAP E3

The most dramatic of the Mayan cities, this has gigantic buildings, including the great pyramid that has become an enduring symbol of the Yucatán *(see pp28–31)*.

7 Tulum
MAP G4

A small city from the last decades of Mayan civilization, Tulum is spectacular as the only Mayan city built above a beach (see pp22–3).

8 Edzná
MAP B5

One of the largest and wealthiest cities of Classic-era Yucatán (see p42), Edzná boasts a huge palace, the "Building of the Five Stories," which is the largest and most complex of all Mayan multistory buildings (see also p39).

9 Uxmal
MAP C4

A hugely atmospheric city, Uxmal has some of the finest Mayan buildings in the Nunnery Quadrangle and the Governor's Palace (see pp34–7).

Pyramid of the Magician, Uxmal

10 Cobá
MAP F3

Before the rise of Chichén Itzá, Cobá was the largest and most powerful city in northern Yucatán. Buildings are spread over a huge area of dense forest and lakes. The Nohoch Mul, at 138 ft (42 m), is the highest pyramid in the Yucatán (see p92).

TOP 10 QUIETER SITES

Aké's strange stone columns

1 El Rey, Cancún
The relics of the historic occupiers of Cancún Island (see p13).

2 El Meco, Cancún
The most important city near Cancún in pre-Hispanic times (see p82).

3 San Gervasio, Cozumel
Capital of the island when it was one of the great pilgrimage centers of Mayan Yucatán (see pp14–15).

4 Xel-Ha
One of the oldest Mayan sites near the modern Riviera, with ancient murals of birds (see p23).

5 Muyil
A very old Mayan site next to the Sian Ka'an reserve, with several pyramids amid the forest (see p26).

6 Aké
MAP C2
Built of massive columns and huge stone slabs, this city is unlike anywhere else in the Yucatán (see 101).

7 Xcambó
MAP C2
A tiny site with a Catholic chapel built onto one of its pyramids (see p104).

8 Oxkintok
MAP B3
Ancient city just west of the Puuc area. It rivalled Uxmal in size, and it has a bizarre temple-labyrinth (see p112).

9 Xlapak
MAP C4
The Palacio has a frieze of elaborately carved Chac-masks (see p112).

10 Mayapán
MAP C3
The last major Mayan city, which dominated the Yucatán from 1200–1400 (see p112).

🔟 Colonial Towns

Valladolid cathedral and main square

1 Valladolid

The city is a combination of distinguished colonial architecture and the easygoing atmosphere of a Yucatán market town. Whitewashed arcades and 17th-century houses surround the main plaza, and among the town's many old Spanish houses and churches is a fine Franciscan monastery (see p48). Just off the plaza, Casa de los Venados houses one of Mexico's finest collections of modern folk art. Four blocks away is the dramatic pit of Cenote Zací, once Valladolid's main source of water.

2 Tizimín

The city's name comes from the Mayan *tsimin*, a kind of demon, also used to describe the Spaniards when they first appeared on horseback. Today the town is the capital of Yucatán's "cattle country," between Valladolid and Río Lagartos. Its pleasant twin central plazas are divided by two huge monasteries, giving it a distinctly Mediterranean appearance (see p104).

3 Teabo
MAP C4

With an air of tranquility, this remote town clusters around its grand and lofty Franciscan church, built in 1650–95. In the sacristy are rare murals of saints, discovered by accident in the 1980s. Teabo is also known for its fine embroidery.

4 Izamal

Known as La Ciudad Dorada, the Golden City, because of the ocher wash of its buildings, this is the most complete and unchanged of Yucatán colonial towns. At its heart is the largest of the Yucatán's Franciscan monasteries (see p48), and a short distance from this are the pyramids of a much older Mayan city. *Victorias*, or horse-drawn carriages, are a favorite way of getting around (see p102).

Horse-drawn carriage, Izamal

Ancient Mayan pyramid, Acanceh

5 Acanceh
MAP C3

An extraordinary little town in which over 2,000 years of time are on show, from its ancient Mayan edifices to a fine 18th-century Spanish church.

6 Ticul

With a slow-moving, unfussy, friendly atmosphere, Ticul is the epitome of a small Yucatán country town and makes an excellent base for visiting the Puuc ruins *(see p37)*. Shoes are the town's traditional product, and it also has a museum dedicated to chocolate, featuring live demonstrations cultural and re-enactments.

7 Oxkutzcab
MAP C4

The south of Yucatán near the Puuc hills is a fertile, fruit-producing region. Oxkutzcab has a huge market, where Mayan women in *huípiles* (white blouses with bright embroidery) preside over stalls stacked with succulent mangoes, papaya, oranges, watermelons, and more. Above them stands the lofty tower of the town church, finished in 1645.

8 Mérida

The capital of the Yucatán, which was founded by the Spaniards in 1542 on the site of the ancient Mayan city of Ti'ho, has a seductive appeal. Whitewashed Spanish houses with shaded patios provide delightful places to stay. Despite the bustle of its market (and traffic), amid the city's old squares daily life still proceeds at a leisurely, friendly pace *(see pp32–3)*.

9 Campeche

The most complete Spanish walled city in Mexico, Campeche is full of reminders of the era when it was a trading hub of Spain's empire and looked upon with greed by Caribbean pirates. The old city – complete with its churches, patios, Andalusian-style grill windows, and facades in delicate pastel colors – has been restored to refresh its distinctive Hispanic character and charm *(see pp38–9)*.

10 Maní
MAP C4

Now wonderfully sleepy, this town was important at the time of the Spanish Conquest, and contains the oldest Franciscan missionary monastery in the Yucatán, the scene of dramatic events in 1562 *(see p48)*. The town was the seat of Tutul Xiu, the first of the Mayan lords to accept Spanish authority in 1542. The monastery and town square are situated on the top of an old Mayan temple-platform.

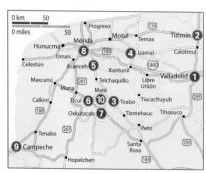

🔟 Churches

1 San Antonio de Padua, Izamal
MAP D2

The vast monastery of Izamal, painted ocher and white like the rest of the town *(see p46)*, epitomizes the plain, austere style favored by the Franciscan friars, who brought Catholicism to the Yucatán. It was founded in 1549, and its huge *atrio*, or court-yard, was designed to hold great crowds of Mayans worshipping in open-air Masses.

2 San Bernardino Sisal, Valladolid
MAP E3

The oldest permanent church in the Yucatán began as part of a Franciscan monastery in 1552. It was located outside Valladolid in order to function both as a place of worship for the Spanish townsfolk and as a mission for Mayan villagers. Inside is a spectacularly painted Baroque altarpiece. The cloister surrounds an overgrown, palm-filled garden with a massive stone well from 1613, built over a cenote *(see p72 and 102)*.

San Bernardino Sisal, Valladolid

3 Maní Monastery
MAP C4

The first of all the Franciscan missionary monasteries in the Yucatán, consecrated in 1549, Maní was built very simply, with a massive stone facade and cavernous cloister. Set within the facade was an external altar or "Indian Chapel," so that open-air services could be held in the square. In 1562, after the Franciscans discovered that many Mayans were practising their old religion in secret, an *auto da fé* was held in the square, during which the friars burned hundreds of Mayan manuscripts and pagan relics *(see p47)*.

Retable carving, Maní Monastery

4 La Mejorada, Mérida
MAP C2

This large church with a very Spanish-looking plain facade was built as part of a major Franciscan friary in 1640. It was the last occupied monastery in Mérida, and closed only in 1857. Behind the church, some of the former monastery buildings now house a school of architecture.

7 Tekax Church
MAP C4

Completed in 1692, this huge yet finely proportioned church was built in a lighter style than those of the early colonial period. The churches at Teabo and Oxkutzcab are similar *(see pp46–7)*.

8 Campeche Cathedral
MAP A5

Mérida and Campeche began their cathedrals around the same time, but the stop-start construction at Campeche meant that while the central façade was finished during the 1600s, the tower on its left was added only in the 1750s, and that on its right as late as the 1850s.

9 Iglesia de Jesús, Mérida
MAP C2

Built for the Jesuit Order and completed in 1618, the Jesús has a gilded Baroque interior that contrasts strikingly with the simplicity of the Franciscan churches. On the exterior, look out for traces of carvings on some of the stones – these were taken from Mayan temples *(see p33)*.

Around Mérida Cathedral

5 Mérida Cathedral
MAP C2

The first cathedral completed in mainland America was built by local conquistadores in a style that the church leaders considered far too extravagant. The design is, in fact, quite simple, with few decorative flourishes, and the church's soaring white stone interior has great solemnity. The figures that you pass on the way in, flanking the imposing main entrance, represent saints Peter and Paul *(see p32)*.

6 Las Monjas, Mérida
MAP C2

The church of "The Nuns" was built in the 1590s as a chapel for one of the first closed convents in the Americas. The castle-like mirador, or watchtower, with its unusual loggia (covered balcony) was built so that the nuns could take the air without leaving the convent. Somber metal grills inside the church recall the separation that was kept between nuns and lay worshippers.

Baroque interior of Iglesia de Jesús

10 San Roque, Campeche
MAP A5

Campeche's churches are generally more colorful than those of Mérida and central Yucatán. San Roque is an extravagant example of Mexican Baroque, with a beautifully restored opulent altarpiece that is surrounded by intricate white plasterwork.

ⓘⓞ Beaches

① Cancún

This resort has the longest stretch of beach, backed by the biggest hotels and malls, and with the most attractions, ranging from parasailing to water parks. The beaches on the north side of the island are the best for swimming and beach-life, but they can get rather crowded. On the surf beaches along the east it is always possible to find a spot to yourself, but check safety conditions (see pp12–13).

Azure waters off Puerto Morelos

② Puerto Morelos

Despite its location between Cancún and Playa del Carmen, Puerto Morelos has avoided big-scale development. There's plenty of space along the long, white beach, where pelicans hang in the wind. A great snorkeling reef (see p52) lies close to the shore (see p79).

③ Cozumel

The island's fan base is split into three: divers, cruise passengers, and families. The finest diving locations are in the distant reefs, but the tranquil beaches along Cozumel's west coast are wonderful for a first experience of snorkeling. San Miguel town has a touristy but easygoing feel (see pp14–15).

Beachgoers at Playa del Carmen

④ Playa del Carmen

This is the fastest-growing and hippest spot on the Mayan Riviera, with good shopping, strolling, bar-hanging, and people-watching opportunities, and miles of lovely palm-lined bays stretching away to the north. To the south, the Playacar development has its own narrower beaches (see pp16–17).

⑤ Isla Mujeres

Isla's small size means it has a more laid-back beach scene, especially on Playa Norte by Isla town, with its placid, safe waters. The island is a good-value diving center (see pp20–21).

⑥ Akumal

This is a lovely area that extends through beautiful, sweeping bays of white sands and gentle seas.

Some big hotels have opened, but secluded and low-key condominium apartments and villas can be found located along most of the bays. Akumal is also an excellent diving center (see p52 and 92).

7 Tulum

The most favored place in the Yucatán for anyone wanting to settle into a palm-roofed cabin by a beach for a while. Head to the north end for cheap cabins where you will get to know your neighbors, or turn south for more seclusion and seductive comforts in some cabins (see pp22–3 and 52).

8 Celestún

Most tourists go to Celestún only to see its flamingos (see p55), but it is also a tranquil village with an endless white-sand beach lined by fishing boats. There are some very enjoyable beach restaurants (see p115) and often wonderful sunsets over the Gulf of Mexico (see p109).

9 Isla Holbox

One of the hippest destinations in the Yucatán, particularly amongst backpackers, Isla Holbox has attractive beaches facing onto the Gulf of Mexico. From May to mid-September the waters offshore are home to endangered whale sharks, which can be spotted on boat and snorkelling trips.

Sailing off Puerto Aventuras

10 Puerto Aventuras

This Mediterranean-style resort town was purpose-built from scratch around a natural inlet in the coast. It now contains the Riviera's best-equipped yachting marina, surrounded by a smart holiday village of villas and condo apartments. There's also a Dolphin Discovery center (see p21), a golf course, tennis center, and several large hotels.

White-sand beach at Isla Holbox

🔟 Diving Reefs

Manchones reef, Isla Mujeres

1 Manchones, Isla Mujeres
MAP L2

A fascinatingly varied reef, half a mile (1 km) long, but only 30 ft (9 m) deep for much of it. The Sac Bajo area, just off the lagoon south of Isla Town, is excellent for snorkeling, and there are spectacular reefs farther from the island (see pp20–21).

2 Tankah
MAP P6

This less well-known beach with just a few hotels is great for relaxed snorkeling and diving away from the crowds. As at Akumal, the reef is quite close to the shore (see p94).

3 Paraíso, Cozumel
MAP R5

Cozumel offers the greatest extent and variety of reef for snorkelers and divers of every level of experience, and visibility is ideal. Paraíso and nearby Chankanaab are "must-sees," with strangely shaped coral just below the surface (see pp14–15).

4 Puerto Morelos
MAP R3

One of the most vibrant of the mainland beaches and officially protected as a *parque marítimo*. The reef is unusually close to the shore, so it is great for snorkel tours and introductory diving. The few dive and snorkel operators here offer a personal, friendly service (see p79).

5 Akumal
MAP P5

The beaches here provide an important breeding area for sea turtles, which coexist with the development along the bays. The reefs fringing the beaches are wonderful for snorkeling and diving (see p92). Akumal is also an important cave-diving center, with Aquatech based at the Villas de Rosa Beach Resort (see p130).

6 Tulum
MAP P6

This is the Riviera's biggest center for cave-diving (see pp58–9), but dive operators also take snorkelers and divers to the reefs nearby, in a deliciously clear sea (see pp22–3).

Cave-diving at Tulum

Reefs around Cancún
MAP K4 & K6

Despite busy beaches and the relatively small size of the closest reefs, there's still lots to see here. "Jungle" snorkeling tours take you through mangroves in Laguna Nichupté and to the reef off Punta Nizuc (see pp12–13).

⑧ Playa del Carmen and Chunzubul
MAP Q4

Several high-standard dive operators are based in Playa, taking divers to the reefs nearby and elsewhere along the Riviera (see pp16–17).

Corals of Palancar, Cozumel

Palancar, Cozumel
MAP Q6

An extraordinary coral mountain with giant canyons that plunge straight from the surface to the depths of the ocean. Nearby, the Yucab and El Cedral reefs are famous for colonies of moray eels and groupers, and tree-like coral heads (see pp14–15).

Xpu-Ha
MAP P5

The superb reefs offshore here are a favorite destination for Playa del Carmen dive operators. Angelfish, triggerfish, and parrotfish are abundant, along with a luxuriant range of coral (see p93).

TOP 10 REEF ANIMALS

1 Fan Corals
Delicately veined fronds coming up from the ocean floor and wave graciously in the undersea currents.

2 Sea Cucumbers
Tube-like creatures with a tough, spiny skin that can be seen lying motionless on the seabed or in clefts in the coral.

3 Snappers
Among the commonest fish here, yellowtail, blackfin, and other snappers move in huge, gleaming shoals.

4 Angelfish
Spectacularly colorful fish, with a fan-like shape and luminous stripes and patches in vibrant yellows and electric blue.

5 Sergeant Majors
Bright, darting little fish, easily recognizable by their black and yellow vertical stripes.

6 Pufferfish
Bizarre fish that, when provoked, inflate themselves by taking in water in order to deter attackers.

7 Parrotfish
These come in many varieties and sizes, but most are very colorful and look as if they are smiling amiably.

8 Rays
Spotted eagle rays, elegantly waving their "wings" as if to fly through the water, are common around some of the Cozumel reefs.

9 Barracudas and Sharks
Many varieties are found around the Yucatán reefs – but attacks on humans are almost unknown.

10 Turtles
Now endangered, sea turtles come ashore to lay their eggs on sandy beaches along the southern Riviera.

Sea turtle

🔟 Wildlife Reserves

Beautiful lagoons of Isla Contoy

1 Isla Contoy
MAP H1

This uninhabited island reserve north of Isla Mujeres is home to a huge range of sea birds, including pelicans, boobies, and frigate birds, and contains mangroves, turtle-breeding beaches, and superb coral lagoons. One-day tours are run by many dive shops and agencies from Isla and Cancún; check what is included in your tour (see p21).

2 Campeche Petenes
MAP A4 ■ Boats can be hired in the village of Isla Arena, and tours are offered in Campeche

The north of Campeche State behind the coast consists of mangrove lagoons and *petenes* – "islands" of solid land within the swamp that have special microclimates all of their own. Within the area are flamingos, deer, and even pumas. Visitor facilities are very limited.

3 Puerto Morelos
MAP R3

The reef off Puerto Morelos is one of the least disturbed sections of coral near the mainland in the northern part of the Maya reef and is now protected as a marine park. Snorkelers can see spectacular marine life – lobsters, giant sponges, luminous parrot fish, and angelfish. Dive operators in the town offer low-impact snorkel and diving tours (see p52).

4 Sian Ka'an Biosphere Reserve
MAP F6

Biggest by far of the Yucatán's nature reserves, this vast expanse of empty forest, mangroves, and lagoons gives an extraordinary glimpse of nature almost untouched by human habitation, and in all

Boat-billed heron, Sian Ka'an

its complexity. Tulum is the starting point for organized trips into the reserve (see pp26–7).

5 Punta Laguna
MAP N4 ■ daily

Spider monkeys are quite common in the Yucatán but often hard to see. Set in very dense forest around a lake near Cobá, this village-run reserve is one of the places to find them. Villagers will guide you to the best spots, and monkeys are most likely to be around in the early morning and early afternoon (see p94).

A flock of flamingos taking off from a creek at Río Lagartos

6 Río Lagartos
MAP F1

A huge, long, narrow lagoon of creeks, mangroves, and mud and salt flats runs along the north coast of Yucatán and it is tinged pink with colonies of 20,000 flamingos in the peak August breeding season. Fascinating, great-value boat trips are run from Río Lagartos and nearby San Felipe *(see p61 and p102)*.

7 Bocas de Dzilam
MAP D1 ■ Boatmen in Río Lagartos, San Felipe, and Dzilam Bravo can be hired to take you to the mangrove lagoons ■ Trips last a full day

Much more remote, this giant expanse of uninhabited mangrove lagoons extends west of San Felipe and also contains flamingo colonies and a variety of birds and other undisturbed wildlife. Getting there, with a boat trip over open sea, is a real adventure.

8 Celestún
MAP A3

The most famous flamingo colonies in the Yucatán are in the lagoon beside this little town on the west coast. Launches run from a visitor center toward the pink streaks of flamingos on the horizon, passing fishermen's huts and ibises and many other birds – an ornithologist's delight *(see p61 and p109)*.

9 Punta Sur Eco Beach Park, Cozumel
MAP R6

This large area across the southern tip of Cozumel has an impressive variety of landscapes – forest, dunes, turtle beaches, reefs, and tranquil mangrove lagoons – plus crocodiles, flamingos, and countless other birds. There are observation towers, an information center, and a maritime museum, and you can climb the Punta Celaraín lighthouse *(see p15)*.

Crocodile, Punta Sur Eco Park, Cozumel

10 Uaymitún
MAP C2 ■ Donations welcomed

For easy bird-watching in the lagoons along the northern Yucatán coast, this free viewing tower by the coast road east of Progreso is a good option; it even provides binoculars. The top offers spectacular views over the wetlands to the south, and you can see flamingos, ducks, egrets, and, in winter, countless migratory birds from North America.

TOP 10 Eco-Parks and Theme Parks

1 Laguna Chankanaab, Cozumel

MAP R5 ■ Open 8am–6pm daily ■ Adm

This small nature and snorkeling park lies close to the Chankanaab and Paraíso reefs (see p52) and includes a beach, a botanical garden, and a Dolphin Discovery center.

2 Aqua World, Cancún

MAP K5 ■ Blvd Kukulcán, km 15.2 ■ (998) 848 8326 ■ Open 7am–8pm daily ■ Charges per activity ■ www.aquaworld.com.mx

A multiactivity fun center on Cancún Island offering jungle tours, submarine rides, jetskiing, snorkeling, diving, fishing, parasailing, dinner cruises, and tours to Isla Mujeres and Cozumel.

Scuba diving at Aqua World

3 Wet'n Wild

MAP J6

Part of the seven "worlds" of Ventura Park Cancun, the biggest water park in town has an interactive dolphin pool, a 350-yd (320-m) lazy river and a kids' pool. But the biggest highlight is the Wet'n Wild water park, with slides, rides, and wave pools for all ages (see p64 and p82).

Parque Garrafón on Isla Mujeres

4 Parque Garrafón, Isla Mujeres

MAP L2 ■ (1) 866 393 5158 ■ Open 8:30am–6:30pm (to 5pm in winter) ■ Adm ■ www.garrafon.com.mx

A broad, natural pool of rock and coral is the central attraction. There's also a swimming pool, and snorkeling reefs just offshore. The calm waters make it good for novices, while hiking and biking trails offer a change of scene.

5 Dos Ojos Cenote

MAP P6 ■ Tours at 9am–4:30pm (to 5pm in winter) ■ Adm ■ www.cenotedosojos.com

The upper chambers of the world's longest underwater cave system, the Dos Ojos Cenote, are used by the diving tours for one of the Yucatán's most exciting tours. Visitors can snorkel or scuba dive through crystal-clear cave waters in giant arched-roof caverns (see p23).

6 Xplor

MAP Q4

Located 4 miles (6 km) south of Playa del Carmen, Xplor is the Riviera Maya's biggest adventure park. No fewer than 14 separate ziplines take visitors soaring above the jungle canopy to splashdown landings in cool, cenote waters. Visitors can drive amphibious vehicles across rope bridges and through grottoes and jungle, paddle a raft on warm, clear waters through subterranean caverns, and swim along underground rivers amid stalactites and stalagmites *(see p80–81)*.

(7) Aktun-Chen
MAP P5 ■ **(984) 109 2061**
■ Open 9am–5:30pm daily ■ Adm (prices vary by activity) ■ www.aktunchen.com

From the highway near Akumal, a dirt track leads west through thick bromeliad-filled jungle to a nature park set around a vast cave and cenote system. Swim and zipline across the cenote and take guided tours through the stalactite-filled cavern, which is highly impressive. Colorful birds, monkeys, and wild boars can be seen outside.

(8) Xel-Ha
MAP P6

One of the Riviera's most popular attractions, this snorkel park was created around a magnificent natural coastal lagoon that's especially good for children. It can seem crowded at first, but if you swim a bit away from the landing stages, you'll still find plenty of fish and coral to admire in peace and quiet. There are also some lovely forest trails to explore *(see p65 and p92)*.

(9) Dolphin Discovery
MAP L1 ■ **(1) 866 393 5158**
■ Timings vary ■ Adm (prices vary by activity) ■ Min age 8 ■ Reservations essential ■ www.dolphindiscovery.com

The region has four of these sea enclosures – at Cozumel, in Tulum-Akumal, on Cancún-Isla Mujeres, and at Costa Maya. Guests can swim or dive with the dolphins, be towed by them, experience the "foot push," and receive hugs from the dolphins.

(10) Xcaret
MAP G3 & Q4

The Riviera's original eco-park provides a spectacular introduction to the richness and variety of a tropical environment *(see pp18–19)*.

Lush natural setting of Xcaret

TOP 10 Cenotes and Caves

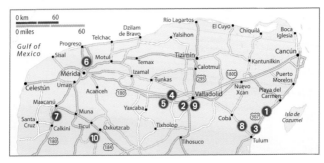

1 Cenote and Eco-park Kantun-Chi

MAP P5

There are several cenotes on the landward side of the highway near Xpu-Ha that can be easily accessed by visitors. A broad, shady pool dappled by brilliant sunlight, Kantun-Chi is near the road but refreshing for swimming. The neighboring cenotes of Cristalino and Azul are also beautiful (see p82).

Cavern-pool of Cenote Samula

2 Cenote Samula

MAP E3 ▪ Dzitnup village ▪ Open 8am–5pm daily ▪ Adm

Past a narrow entrance there's a huge pool of cool, clear water and, in the cave, the roots of a giant ceiba tree – associated with mystical powers by the Maya – stretch straight down from the surface to reach the water far below.

3 Dos Ojos Cenote

MAP P6

This cavern is called "Two Eyes" because its two entrances look like eyes when seen from above. Extending over 350 miles (563 km) through a labyrinth of caverns and limestone "trees," it has been considered the world's longest underwater cave system – but the nearby Nohoch Nah Chich cenote may be even longer. Inexperienced divers get most from it with the diving tours (see p56).

4 Balankanché Caves

MAP E3 ▪ Open daily, guided tours only ▪ Adm

Alongside several cenote pools and underwater rivers, the Yucatán is underlain by a massive web of dry caves that were sacred places to the ancient Maya. Balankanché, near Chichén Itzá, is one of the largest and most extraordinary cave systems of all (see p100).

5 Sacred Cenote, Chichén Itzá

MAP E3 ▪ Adm as for Chichén Itzá

The most celebrated cenote in the Yucatán, the giant sacred well at Chichén (see p29) has long been said to have been a place of human sacrifice. The cenote was used only for ritual purposes, perhaps as a channel to the Underworld, since the city's drinking water came from the Xtoloc Cenote, near the Caracol.

⑥ Cenote Xlacah, Dzibilchaltún

MAP C2 ▪ Open 8am–5pm daily ▪ Adm

The wide cenote that provided water for the ancient city of Dzibilchaltún is still a popular swimming hole today. It gets busy on Sundays but is great for a dip at other times *(see p110)*.

⑦ Calcehtok

MAP B3

These little-known caves near the Mayan ruins at Oxkintok *(see p112)* are some of the region's most extraordinary. The roofless main chamber is big enough to contain whole trees, and is full of birds.

⑧ Gran Cenote

MAP N6 ▪ Open 8am–5pm daily ▪ Adm

The loveliest of several cenotes along the road from Tulum to Cobá, Gran Cenote has a placid, clear pool. Snorkelers and divers can make their way through a massive arched cavern and down a tunnel.

⑨ Cenote Dzitnup

MAP E3 ▪ Dzitnup village, 3 miles (5 km) W of Valladolid ▪ Open 8am–5pm daily ▪ Adm

The most famous swimmable cenote, this awe-inspiring limestone cathedral, with a perfect turquoise pool, is entered via a narrow tunnel. Tours visit at about 11am, but at other times it's rarely crowded *(see p101)*.

Dramatic Loltún Caves

⑩ Loltún Caves

MAP C4 ▪ Open daily; guided tours only ▪ Adm

An astonishing cave system not far from the Puuc cities *(see p37)*, with the longest history of human habitation in the Yucatán. Chambers are full of bizarre rock formations, strange airflows, and relics of their Mayan occupants *(see p111)*.

Cenote Dzitnup's perfect pool

🔟 Off the Beaten Path

Punta Allen's peaceful beach

1 Punta Allen
MAP G5

The atrocious state of the road keeps visitor numbers down, but the trek deep into Sian Ka'an (four-wheel-drive only) takes you to a tiny fishing village of sand streets and giant palms, with landing stages by the beach and a few easy-going restaurants and welcoming places to stay. Local guides offer snorkeling, bird-watching, and fishing trips (see p21).

2 Río Lagartos and San Felipe
MAP E–F1

Celebrated for the spectacular flocks of flamingos in the lagoon to their east (see p55), these villages delight visitors with their unhurried, easy-going style. There are great seafood restaurants too, as well as some pleasant small hotels, and, from San Felipe, wonderful sunsets (see p55 and pp102–3).

3 Puerto Morelos
MAP R3

An undisturbed gem of the Mexican Caribbean, Puerto Morelos has kept its mellow, fishing-village feel despite its close proximity to Cancún. There is no real nightlife to be found here, but there are lovely beaches, and many small apartments and hotels here offer long-term rates (see p54 and p80).

4 Punta Bete
MAP R4

A well-rutted track off the main highway just north of Playa del Carmen leads in 2 bumpy miles (3 km) to superb, curving beaches of dazzling white sand and a perfect turquoise sea. Some resort hotels have opened up here, but there are still clusters of laid-back beach cabañas (see p129) tucked away among the palms (see p80).

Tranquil lagoon of Río Lagartos and San Felipe

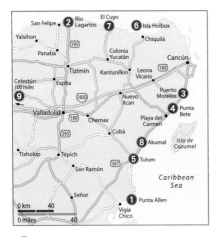

often occupied only by a few small-scale hotels and condo apartments. It's quite easy to find uncrowded space at Akumal, by an idyllic sea and with creature comforts included. There are also excellent diving facilities to be found here (see p88).

9 Celestún
MAP A2

Flamingos, again, are the big attraction here but, if you stay over in one of the small hotels after the day-trippers have returned to Mérida, you will be able to make the most of a delightfully peaceful little village, its beach strewn with fishing boats (see p55 and 109). North of Celestún is a really remote beach retreat at Xixim (see p129).

5 Tulum
MAP P6

The epitome of a tropical paradise: palm-shaded cabins only a few steps from a vividly colored sea, and with just candlelight and the sound of waves at night. The bargain cabañas at the north end of the beach are slightly noisier, so head south for pure tranquility (see pp22–3).

6 Isla Holbox
MAP G1

If the Riviera seems just too busy, take a long drive north to the tiny port of Chiquilá. Hop on a ferry to cross the beautiful lagoon (where dolphins are common) to reach the island of Holbox. Here you'll find the simple pleasures of a friendly village, a long, empty beach, and some mellow places to stay (see p51 and p83).

7 El Cuyo
MAP F1

With just one hotel, two sets of beach cabañas, and a couple of places to eat – with great fresh fish – this Gulf coast fishing village is for anyone who really does want a beach all to themselves (see p104).

8 Akumal
MAP P5

Not a remote spot, but the curving beaches here are very long and

Pool at the Temozon Hacienda hotel

10 Hacienda Hotels

A seductive escape is offered (at upscale prices) by the hotels scattered around the Yucatán in beautifully converted old colonial haciendas (country estates). All have luxurious rooms surrounded by tropical gardens, with superb pools and fine restaurants (see pp127–8).

🔟 Sports and Activities

Spectacular bird's-eye view of a golf course in Cancún's Hotel Zone

① Golf
Club de Golf Cancún: (998) 883 1230 ▪ Puerto Aventuras Golf Club: (984) 873 5109 ▪ Palace Resort (01) 800 635 1836; www.palaceresorts.com
Golfers on the Riviera have a choice of two championship-level courses at Cancún, one in Playacar and one at Puerto Aventuras. Hotels can book greens for you. North of Mérida there is also a private club, which can be booked through hotels.

② Sailing, Windsurfing, and Kayaking
Aqua World: (998) 848 8327; www.aquaworld.com.mx
The best places to rent boats are Isla Mujeres and Cozumel. Hotels may

Kayaking on the Riva Maya

have dinghies available for use by guests. A day's sailing is a great way to explore lesser-known stretches of the coast. Windsurfing is at its finest around Isla Mujeres and Akumal, and the best spots for kayaking are around Puerto Morelos and Punta Solimán (see p95).

③ Diving
Scuba Cancun: (998) 849 7508; www.scubacancun.com.mx
The Mayan Riviera is the site of the second-largest reef in the world. Scuba Cancun offers diving opportunities in Cancún, Riviera Maya, and Cozumel.

④ Fishing
Conditions for deep-sea and inshore fishing in the Yucatán are outstanding, and the lagoons south of the Riviera by Ascencion Bay are a must for fly-fishing fans. The peak deep-sea fishing season runs from March to June.

⑤ Tennis
RIU Caribe Hotel: (998) 848 7850 ▪ Hotel Omni: (998) 848 7850
Many resort hotels have tennis courts. In Cancún, Hotel Omni's courts are open to all, while those at RIU Caribe Hotel are for residents only. The Club de Golf Cancún also has two courts.

6 Cycling

The most attractive towns for cycling are Cancún, Isla Mujeres, Tulum, and Valladolid, which has a lovely cycle path to Cenote Dzitnup (see p59). Many Cancún hotels have bikes, and there are rental shops in the other three destinations.

7 Skydiving

Sky Dive Playa: (984) 873 0192; www.skydive.com.mx

Sky Dive Playa will offer visitors a bird's-eye view of the Riviera as they plummet down harnessed to an instructor, or on their own if they have skydiving experience.

8 Air Tours

Aerosaab: (998) 865 4225; www.aerosaab.com ■ Fly Tours Cancun: flytourscancun.com

Aerosaab at Playa del Carmen and Fly Tours Cancún at Cancún offer aerial sightseeing tours over the Riviera, Chichén Itzá, and other parts of the Yucatán Peninsula.

Parasailing over Cancún

9 Parasailing

Soar above Cancún with the "Skyrider" at Aqua World. More basic operations are to be found at Cancún beach and at Playa del Carmen.

10 Jungle Tours

Alltournative (888): 844 5010, www.alltournative.com ■ ATV Explorer: (984) 873 1626; www. ATVExplorer.com

Playa-based ATV Explorer let you race through the jungle on four-wheel ATVs. Alltournative runs group trips by truck, jeep, and kayak.

TOP 10 FISHING LOCATIONS

Fishing boats in Puerto Morelos

1 Cancún
For easy-access, fun fishing, with trips available from water sports centers such as Aqua World (see p56).

2 Isla Mujeres
Highly regarded by deep-sea fishing enthusiasts, with able captains who seek out amberjack, marlin, and more.

3 Cozumel
A base for many expert deep-sea captains, who also offer trips to the inshore flats.

4 Puerto Morelos
Much lower key than the islands, but deep water close to shore means superb fishing.

5 Playa del Carmen
Many Playa dive shops also arrange fishing trips, especially in the sailfishing season (March–June).

6 Puerto Aventuras
The most luxuriously equipped fishing center on the coast. Hosts a big deep-sea tournament each May.

7 Boca Paila and Punta Allen
Fly-fishing and, above all, bonefish followers make their way to the remote fishing lodges along this road.

8 Isla Holbox
A long way from the conveniences of the Riviera, but loved by fishermen who like a really relaxing time.

9 El Cuyo
The one bar, La Conchita, is the place to go to find a boat and a guide. Shark fishing is a specialty of the north coast.

10 Río Lagartos
No well-organized facilities here, but boatmen will show you their fishing grounds as well as the flamingo lagoons.

🔟 Children's Attractions

1 Wet'n Wild, Cancún
MAP J6 ■ Boulevard Kukulcán, km 25 ■ (998) 193 2000 ■ Open 10am–5pm daily ■ Adm ■ www. wetnwildcancun.com

The number one fun center in the region. As well as the adrenaline-pumping rides that older kids love – the Wave Pool, Bubba Tub, Kamikaze, Double Space Bowl, and Twister, Wet'n Wild also has a Kids' Park with rides and slides for young children, so that even the littlest members of the family can join in the fun (see p56 and p82).

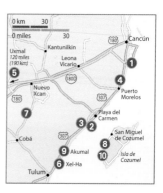

Families snorkeling at Xcaret

2 Xcaret
MAP Q4 ■ (998) 251 6560 ■ Open 8:30am–10:30pm daily ■ Adm ■ www.xcaret.com

The first and most famous of the eco-parks provides lots for kids to enjoy, in an easy, family-centered environment. The snorkeling river and dolphin pool are the biggest hits, but children can also enjoy the zoo, butterfly garden, and forest paths (see pp18–19).

3 Río Secreto
MAP Q4 ■ (984) 877 2377 ■ www.riosecreto.com

This amazing underground cave and river system is located just south of Playa del Carmen. Don a wet suit and helmet to explore the river that flows 82 ft (25 m) below the surface and see the many spectacular stalagmites and stalactites.

4 Crococún Crocodile Park
MAP R3 ■ Highway 307, km 31 ■ (998) 850 3719 ■ Open 9am–5pm daily ■ Adm $30 (60yrs & above $18; under 6s free) ■ www.crococunzoo.com

Kids meet crocs (over 300 of them) at this attractive small zoo of all-local wildlife. Multilingual guides give informative, entertaining tours, and there are opportunities to pet and feed baby crocodiles, deer, monkeys, parrots, and less familiar animals such as tepezcuintles (an endearing, large spotted rodent).

5 Uxmal
MAP C4

Some kids love Mayan sites; others don't. One that frequently scores a hit is Uxmal. Not only does it have lots of steps and temples for running around, but it is also home to many iguanas, which sit stock still until surprised, then dart off with sudden alacrity. Some are as big as crocodiles, but they're all harmless (see pp34–7).

6 Xel-Ha

MAP P6 ■ (998) 251 6560
■ Open 9am–6pm daily ■ Adm
■ www.xelha.com

This snorkel park is another of the
Riviera's big family attractions. Few
kids are not enchanted by swimming
and snorkeling in the coral lagoon,
as well as by exploring its lush forest
setting (see p92).

7 Punta Laguna

MAP N4 ■ daily

Getting to see local wildlife in its
natural habitat, rather than in zoos
or nature parks, can take time and
effort, but at this small reserve north
of Cobá village guides lead the way
and you can see spider monkeys
jumping through the trees after just
a little exciting exploration. Deer, wild
boar, and lots of birds can likely be
seen too (see p54 and p94).

8 Laguna Chankanaab, Cozumel

MAP R5 ■ Open 8am–4pm daily
■ Adm

One of the most enjoyable and
accessible places for even small
children to be dazzled by a first
introduction to snorkeling and the
underwater treasures of the Cozumel
reefs. The sea is very placid, and
there's coral and abundant sea life
just off the beach. In the same park
there's also a coral lagoon and a
Dolphin Discovery center (see p56).

Children playing at Playa Mia

9 Laguna Yal-Ku, Akumal

MAP P5 ■ Open 8am–6pm
daily ■ Adm

This winding rock pool of brilliant
turquoise water right at the north
end of Akumal's Media Luna Bay is
one of the natural coral inlets on
the Riviera coast. Rarely crowded,
it's delightful for swimming and
snorkeling with young children, with
coral and colorful fish that are easy
to spot.

Rock pool at Laguna Yal-Ku, Akumal

10 Playa Mia, Cozumel

MAP R6 ■ Open dawn–dusk
daily ■ Adm

Cozumel's beach clubs offer all
the fun of the sand and sea, plus
restaurants and loungers in the
shade. Playa Mia has the best choice
of things to do for older children –
snorkeling, beach games, kayaks,
and banana boats – and it has a Kids'
Club for little ones.

📟 **Nightspots**

① Señor Frog's, Cancún
MAP L4

As the sun goes down, Señor Frog's transforms from a restaurant into one of Cancún's most famous nightspots. Daily live music, DJs, and karaoke create a party atmosphere in which to dance the night away. Not to be missed is the water slide that runs from the venue to the lagoon, so make sure you come prepared with your swimwear. Open until the early hours of the morning *(see p86)*.

Vibrant interior of Señor Frog's

② La Santanera, Playa del Carmen
MAP Q4

Centrally located in Playa del Carmen, this club features two separate levels playing different sounds (electronica downstairs, house music upstairs). It's a fun place for all ages, who come here to dance, drink, and enjoy the ambience *(see p85)*.

③ Batey, Tulum
MAP P6 ■ Calle Cenauro ■ (984) 143 3616

A colorfully painted Volkswagen Beetle that has been converted into a *guarapo* (sugarcane) press stands outside this cool bar. Located just off Tulum's main drag, Batey offers perfectly mixed mojitos. In the evenings there are tapas-style snacks and live bands.

④ Blue Parrot Beach Club, Playa del Carmen
MAP Q4

Playa del Carmen has changed enormously since its original beach bar opened in the early 1990s, but the Parrot still remains the number one place to meet up and mingle. There's always a buzzing scene, and you get a fabulous view of the moon over the sea *(see p85)*.

⑤ Dinner Cruises, Cancún
MAP K3 ■ Cancún Lovers, Marina Aquatours, Blvd Kukulcán km 6.25 ■ (998) 193 3370

For a slightly more sedate time try another Cancún specialty, with live shows, games, dinner, and dancing to live bands as you sail around Laguna Nichupté or to Isla Mujeres. Each one is themed: Cancún Queen from Aqua World *(see p56)* is like an old sternwheeled riverboat, the Cancún Lovers Cruise is on a replica Columbus-era galleon, and Captain Hook's Pirate Night is, of course, on a pirate ship *(see p85)*.

⑥ Carlos'n Charlie's, Cozumel
MAP R5

Enjoyable, crowd-pleasing food and a non-stop, bright and breezy party atmosphere are the keys to the success of the Anderson group's bar-restaurants, found all around Mexico under several jokey names – Carlos'n Charlie's, Senor Frog's, and El Shrimp Bucket. This Cozumel branch in Punta Langosta mall is one of the biggest *(see p97)*.

Carlos'n Charlie's, Cozumel

7 Diablito Cha Cha Cha, Playa del Carmen
MAP Q4

At this stylish lounge, black and white floor tiles contrast with red and green furniture – an allusion to the Mexican flag colors. While you sip a vanilla martini and snack on Asian-style seafood the eclectic music ranges from rockabilly to electronica to homegrown pop *(see p86)*.

8 Pancho's, Mérida
MAP C2

Nightlife in Mérida is much more low-key than on the Riviera, but Pancho's, with its Mexican-bandit theme, is consistently the most enjoyable venue in the middle of town. Lively socializing is helped along by the fast and friendly staff, and, at the back, there's a dance floor under the stars *(see p114)*.

Performance at Dady'O, Cancún

9 Coco Bongo, Cancún
MAP L4

The most state-of-the-art of all Cancún's mega-clubs, Coco Bongo is a vast, multilevel, multispace venue with music that covers all the bases – techno, rock, Latin – from DJs and live bands. There is also a space to eat. House specialties include ultraextravagant theme nights, live shows, and other eye-popping surprises *(see p85)*.

10 Dady'O, Cancún
MAP L4

Always the most popular among American student "spring breakers," this equally huge venue across the street from the Coco Bongo guarantees a noisy, down-home party atmosphere – theme parties are a permanent feature. Next door, the only slightly smaller Sweet is a live venue with a bar-restaurant, plus more fun and games *(see p85)*.

The exterior of the famed Coco Bongo nightclub in Cancún

:TOP10: Dishes of the Yucatán

Spicy *cochinita pibil*

① Cochinita Pibil
This punchy dish dates back to pre-Conquest Mayan cooking – pork marinated in lime, bitter orange, and *achiote* (a hot, spicy mix of dried herbs), wrapped in banana leaves and baked in an earthenware dish. A flavorful food, it's very versatile and can be served as a main course or used to fill tacos. *Pollo pibil* is a chicken version of this dish.

② Puchero
Commonly eaten as a Sunday lunch, *puchero* is a heart stew found across Latin America, but with its origins in Spain. In the Yucatán Peninsula it is typically packed with pork, beef, chicken, and vegetables, spiced with allspice and cinnamon, and finished off with a garnish of diced habañero peppers, oranges, coriander, and radishes.

③ Poc-Chuc
Marinating is one of the most characteristic skills of Yucatecan cooking, and this delicious dish features pork marinated in the juice of *naranja agria* (small, bitter oranges, special to the region), cooked with onions, herbs, and garlic, and served with black beans. With a wonderful mix of sweet and savory flavors, it's very popular, but debate rages as to whether it is really traditional or a creation of La Chaya Maya restaurant in Mérida *(see p71).*

④ Pollo Oriental de Valladolid
The pride of Valladolid: chicken quartered on the bone and casseroled with garlic, onion, cloves, and a mix of both hot and mild chilis; it's then quickly roasted in a baste of maize oil and bitter orange juice. This is another regional dish with a rich, densely layered combination of different flavors. *Pavo oriental* is the turkey version.

⑤ Relleno Negro
Yucatecan cooking likes rich concoctions. In *relleno negro* ("black stuffing"), finely ground pork, peppers, grated hard-boiled egg, herbs, spices, and a powerful combination of chilis are mixed together to make up a thick, majestic sauce. It is usually served with turkey *(pavo or guajolote)*, the region's most traditional meat.

Classic *pollo con mole*

⑥ Pollo con Mole
This is a central Mexican classic. Fried chicken is covered in *mole*, a thick, spicy, savory – not at all sweet – chocolate sauce. Richly satisfying, this is one of the oldest uses of chocolate, its flavor uniting perfectly with strongly spiced meats.

7 Crepas de Chaya

Tasting rather like spinach, *chaya* is a vegetable native to the Yucatán. It features in traditional cooking and contemporary dishes such as this one. It is cooked with garlic and wrapped in light, European-style wheat pancakes (crêpes) and served with a cheese sauce. *Chaya* is also used to make drinks (see p71).

Camarón al mojo de ajo

8 Camarón al Mojo de Ajo

All around the coasts, fish and seafood are restaurant staples. One of the simplest and most delicious ways of cooking the likes of *camarón* (prawns/shrimp) and *caracol* (conch) is *al mojo de ajo*, fried quickly in hot oil and lots of garlic.

9 Sopa de Lima

One of the most popular classics of Yucatecan cooking, "lime soup" is actually made with chicken, boned, chopped into strips, and then slow-cooked with coriander, onions, herbs, spices, and masses of local sweet limes. It's served with strips of dry tortillas for added crunch.

10 Arroz con Pulpo

A Campeche specialty: a delicious warm salad that's much lighter than many local dishes on a hot day. Rice *(arroz)* is mixed together with chopped octopus *(pulpo)*, red peppers, onion, coriander, and other herbs, plus, often, mango, papaya, or other fruits, in a refreshing blend of sweet juice and salty seafood flavors.

TOP 10 YUCATECAN SNACKS AND STREET FOODS

1 Ceviche
Raw fish or seafood marinated in lemon or lime juice, and served with salad, spices, and lots of coriander.

2 Cócteles
Usually, fish or seafood ceviches served in a glass accompanied by a vinaigrette-style dressing.

3 Papadzules
A Mayan dish of chopped hard-boiled eggs in a sweet pumpkin-seed sauce, rolled in tortillas and often served with a spicy tomato sauce.

4 Panuchos
Small, crisp-fried tortillas covered in refried beans and topped with strips of chicken or turkey, plus generous helpings of chopped tomato, onion, avocado, and chilis.

5 Salbutes
Similar to *panuchos*, but made with a thicker, spongier base instead of crisp tortillas.

6 Enchiladas
In southern Mexico, these rolled soft tortillas with various fillings tend to be served with a rich *mole* sauce.

7 Tacos
Small rolled tortillas filled with 1,001 possible fillings: at taco stands, they're served rolled up; at *taquerías* you sit and assemble them yourself.

8 Fajitas
Pan-fried meat or seafood served sizzling alongside bowls of onions, refried beans, chili sauce, guacamole, and soft tortillas.

9 Quesadillas
Small, soft tortillas that are folded over and filled with melted cheese and sometimes ham, and served up with a range of sauces.

10 Tortas
Small bread rolls, available with as many different fillings as tacos.

Stuffed quesadillas

🔟 Restaurants

The pleasant courtyard dining space of La Habichuela in Cancún

① La Habichuela, Cancún
Superb Yucatecan and Mexican cooking, well presented with original touches and served in the tranquil setting of a lush garden. Campeche dishes include *cocobichuela*, shrimp and lobster in curry sauce served with coconut rice (see p87).

② El Marlin Azul, Mérida
It's easy to walk past this seafood restaurant and miss it. Look for a blue awning and a crowd of regulars perched at the counter – they're enjoying some of the best seafood in the city, trucked in daily direct from Celestún (see p115).

③ Los Pelícanos, Puerto Morelos
Set beneath a giant *palapa* palm roof, in a spot above the beach, this easygoing local institution serves some of the best ceviches you'll find, as well as grander seafood dishes (see p87).

④ Kinich, Izamal
Tucked into a secluded garden near the largest of Izamal's Mayan pyramids, this is the place to sample the full range of Yucatecan cooking – *cochinita*, *pavo en relleno negro*, and a fragrant *sopa de lima* (see p107).

⑤ La Parrilla, Cancún
At this restaurant, Mexican art and music create an atmospheric setting for delicious local specialties, including Mayan dishes. A warm ambience, great food, and affordable prices have turned La Parrilla into a successful formula exported to other centers along the Riviera (see p87).

⑥ Hartwood, Tulum
Everything is cooked over an open fire at this hip restaurant, run by a former New York restaurateur with a focus on sustainable, eco-friendly cuisine. The tasty, creative menu changes every day, depending on what produce is available and in season (see p99).

Outdoor dining at Hartwood, Tulum

Casa de Piedra, Xcanatún

Yucatecan and Caribbean traditions and ingredients are combined with sophisticated international styles by a French-trained chef: a delicate *sopa de lima* is a menu fixture, alongside the chef's own interesting creations, such as cream of *poblano* chili soup with roquefort (*see p115*).

8 Ku'uk, Mérida

Set in one of Mérida's grand mansions, Ku'uk is a worthy splurge with a great value haute cuisine tasting menu. Chef Pedro Evia uses traditional ingredients and local produce to create innovative dishes that make for an unforgettable experience. The regularly changing menu is complemented with sophisticated cocktails (*see p114*).

Interior of La Chaya Maya

9 La Chaya Maya, Mérida

A cheerful and very popular restaurant, specializing in Yucatecan cuisine. Serving staff in traditional Mayan dress serve up local dishes such as *puchero*, *poc-chuc*, and *sopa de lima* (*see pp68–9*). There are two branches in the city centre (*see p115*).

10 La Pigua, Campeche

The best seafood restaurant in the city offers an attractive dining room, immaculate service, and an appealing menu featuring coconut prawns, octopus in a garlic sauce, and freshly-caught fish in a variety of sauces (*see p99*).

TOP 10 BREAKFASTS AND JUICES

Huevos Motuleños

1 Huevos Rancheros
A breakfast classic: tortillas topped by fried eggs, covered in spicy tomato sauce, and served with refried beans.

2 Huevos Motuleños
As above, but with the addition of peas, ham, and grated cheese, often served with slices of fried banana.

3 Huevos Revueltos
Scrambled eggs, nearly always mixed with a little onion and red pepper, or with ham (*con jamón*).

4 Huevos a la Mexicana
Spicy scrambled eggs with peppers, chili, chopped onions, and chorizo.

5 Chilaquiles
Crisp tortilla chips, baked in a cheese sauce with tomato, onions, herbs, chili, and shredded chicken or turkey.

6 Platillo de Fruta
A big plate of fresh fruit, usually including at least pineapple, watermelon, oranges, bananas, and papaya.

7 Agua de Jamaica
An enormously refreshing local product – an infusion of dried flowers of jamaica (a kind of hibiscus), diluted to make a delicious tall drink.

8 Agua de Chaya
Another infusion, this one of the vegetable *chaya* (*see p69*), best mixed with water and a little squeeze of lemon juice.

9 Licuados
Any kind of fruit, such as watermelon, papaya, pineapple, or mamey, pulped and diluted with water and ice.

10 Raspados
Vibrant fruit juices in crushed ice, packed right to the top of the glass.

For a key to restaurant price ranges see p87

🔟 Cancún and the Yucatán for Free

San Bernadino Sisal altarpiece

1 San Bernardino Sisal, Valladolid

MAP E3 ■ Parque de San Bernardino
■ Open 9am–8pm Wed–Mon

This elegant Franciscan church and former convent has a magnificent 18th-century altarpiece, while the walls are covered with evocative 17th-century paintings (see p48).

2 MACAY, Mérida

MAP C2 ■ Pasaje de la Revolución ■ Open 10am–6pm Wed–Mon
■ www.macay.org

The Museo de Arte Contemporáneo Ateneo de Yucatán (MACAY) is home to an outstanding modern art collection, featuring works by leading Yucatécan painters such as Fernando Castro Pacheco and Fernando García Ponce (see pp32–3).

3 Nightlife in Mérida

MAP C2

Each night of the week the city centre plays host to a range of live music, dance events, theatrical performances, film screenings, and other entertainment. Check out the latest schedule at the city's tourist office (see pp32–3).

4 Izamal's Crafts Workshops

MAP D2 ■ Various locations around town ■ Most workshops open from around 10am–2pm & 4–7pm daily

This small town is famous for its crafts scene, and its woodcarvers, jewelers, hammock-makers, and other artisans are happy to show tourists round their workshops. A free map showing the locations of many of the workshops is available from most hotels in town (see p103 and p105).

5 Palacio Centro Cultural, Campeche

MAP A5 ■ Parque Principal ■ Open 10am–7pm Tue–Sun ■ (981) 816 7741

Charting the tempestuous history of Campeche, this museum offers multimedia displays and innovative exhibits, including a replica Spanish galleon. Most of the descriptions are in Spanish, though a few are also translated into English. There's also a spectacular music and light show on weekends (see pp38–9).

Palacio Centro Cultural, Campeche

6 Xlapak
MAP C4

The smallest and least visited of the Ruta Puuc archaeological sites, the Mayan ruins of Xlapak feature a restored palace with doorways decorated with large, eye-catching Chac (the rain god) masks *(see p112)*.

7 Oxkutzcab Market
MAP C4 ▪ From 7am daily

This charming colonial-era town, surrounded by fruit and vegetable farms, hosts in its main square one of the liveliest and most colourful markets in the region.

8 Punta Bete Beach
MAP R4

This is one of the most picturesque stretches of sand on the Riviera Maya, and less crowded than many of its neighbors thanks to a bumpy access road *(see p60)*.

Yucatán Carnival performers

9 Carnival

Although it's not quite on the scale of its more famous Brazilian counterpart, carnival in Mexico is still a lively and raucous affair. Cancún, Cozumel, and Mérida host the biggest celebrations in the Yucatán region – expect costumed dancers, live music, and plenty of good food and drink. Carnival takes place in the week before Lent *(see p74)*.

10 Mérida Cathedral
MAP C2

Dating back to the late 16th century, Mérida's imposing cathedral is one of the oldest in Latin America *(see pp32–3)*.

TOP 10 BUDGET TIPS

Tasty street food bargains

1 Visit in the low-season: May–June and late November–early December offer the best combinations of prices and weather.

2 The extensive public bus system is an inexpensive way to travel around the region.

3 It is cheaper to rent a car at one of the small agencies in Mérida than in Cancún.

4 Save money by using pesos rather than US dollars.

5 Local free magazines often have discount coupons for hotels, restaurants, and other attractions.

6 Some national monuments offer free admission for Mexican nationals on Sundays, and general admission to museums and historic sites is generally cheaper for Mexican residents.

7 Markets and snack stands are the cheapest and often the most atmospheric places to eat.

8 Cut costs for trips and tours by getting a group together.

9 Most diving operators offer discounts for group or advance bookings, or if you book several dives at the same time.

10 Most Riviera Maya bars offer two-for-one deals for at least a few hours each night.

Mexican currency

🔟 Festivals

① Feast of Three Kings, Tizimín

MAP F2 ▪ Two weeks from Jan 6

The capital of Yucatán's cattle country hosts one of the region's biggest fiestas. It features a stock fair as well as bullfights, traditional music, dancing, colorful parades, and plenty of eating and drinking.

② La Candelaria

MAP E3 ▪ 12 days around Feb 2

Valladolid's main fiesta, the Expo-Feria centers around the Feast of the Virgin of La Candelaria. Local girls show off dazzling embroidered dresses in the opening parade, followed by dancing and free concerts and shows. Campeche has a smaller celebration.

③ Carnival

About one week before Lent

The biggest and brightest celebration of the year in the Yucatán. In Cancún and Cozumel the streets fill with music, dancing, food stands, and a little Río-style parading. The biggest Carnival in southern Mexico, though, is in Mérida.

④ Equinoxes, Chichén Itzá and Dzibilchaltún

Mar 21, Sep 21

The visual effects integral to these Mayan cities – such as the "descent" of the sun down the serpents on El Castillo at Chichén and the striking of the rising sun through the Seven Dolls temple at Dzibilchaltún – were timed to happen on the spring and fall equinoxes. Today, some 80,000 visit Chichén Itza for the day; the crowds are smaller at Dzibilchaltún *(see p29 and p110)*.

Cancún Jazz Festival

⑤ Cancún Jazz Festival

Check website for festival dates (www.cancunjazz.com)

An innovative mix of young artists from Latin America, the U.S., and Europe – often playing Latin Jazz and contemporary fusion rather than strict jazz – features in this festival. Several acts play for free in Parque de las Palapas in Ciudad Cancún.

⑥ San Miguel Arcángel, Cozumel

MAP H3–4 ▪ Sep 20–29

Cozumel's most important traditional fiesta takes place in honor of the island's patron saint, St. Michael. Over the 9 days that precede his feast day, religious processions are held in town, and there's a variety of kids' entertainment, plus free music and dancing.

Equinox at Chichén Itza

7 Cristo de las Ampollas, Mérida

MAP C2 ▪ Week before Oct 13

More solemnly religious than most fiestas, with processions culminating on October 13, when the figure of "Christ of the Blisters" (*Cristo de las Ampollas*), kept in Mérida Cathedral, is carried through town before a Mass.

8 Day of the Dead and All Saints' Day

Oct 31–Nov 2

Sugar skulls, dead bread (*pan de muerto*), zempazuchitl flowers, and coffin-shaped decorations are the mark of Mexico's most famous celebration, when people party to honor the dead on Halloween and All Saints' Day (*Todos Santos*), and families visit cemeteries to picnic by the graves of their departed relatives.

Day of the Dead sugar skulls for sale

9 Mérida en Domingo

MAP C2 ▪ Every Sun

Every week, Mérida hosts a free fiesta, "Mérida on Sunday," when the Plaza Mayor and Calle 60 are closed to traffic to make way for strolling crowds and a range of events. There are displays of *jarana* dancing in front of the City Hall and concerts up and down the street, and anyone can dance, too.

10 Village Fiestas

Every village and town in the Yucatán also has its own fiesta, when the streets are covered in bright garlands, work ceases, and music is heard non-stop. To find out if and when any are due to take place near you, ask in tourist offices, look out for posters, or check local papers.

TOP 10 TRADITIONAL CRAFTS AND PRODUCTS

Colorful hammocks for sale

1 Hammocks
The traditional place to sleep is so much a part of the Yucatán that local poets have even celebrated it in verse.

2 Embroidery
Lush flower designs are made by Mayan women on traditional *huipil* blouses, handkerchiefs, tablecloths, and other linen.

3 Panama Hats
The best palm hats are said to be from northern Campeche, and the place to buy them is Mérida.

4 Guayaberas
These are light, elegant shirts. They are accepted as tropical formal wear and bestow instant dignity upon men (of any age).

5 Sandals
Huge racks of traditional leather *huarache* sandals can be found in all Yucatán markets.

6 Wood Carving
Many Mayan villagers carve wooden figures based on ancient images.

7 *Jícaras* (Gourds)
Dried natural gourd bowls, brightly painted, are a specialty of Chiapas, but they are often seen in the Yucatán.

8 Silverwork and Jewelry
Fine silverware from Taxco in central Mexico is found in Yucatán stores, as well as amber from Chiapas.

9 Painted Birds and Ornaments
Brightly painted wooden parrots, toucans, and boxes provide some of the prettiest images of tropical Mexico.

10 Ceramics
Huge numbers of earthenware pots are made in Ticul, sometimes using pre-Conquest techniques.

Cancún and the Yucatán Area by Area

The Mayan temple-pyramid, El Castillo,
overlooking Tulum's lovely beaches

TOP 10 Cancún and the North

Cancún is the great magnet at the top of the Mayan Riviera, with lavish hotels, shopping and dining of every kind, wild nightclubs, theme parks, water parks, and other entertainment spread out along one of the world's finest beaches. To the south is Playa del Carmen, a trendier, more compact vacation town, and family-friendly eco-parks that provide an unforgettable introduction to the nature of tropical Yucatán. For a change from resort life, in the same area there are also places where the frenetic pace of modern life still seems delightfully far away – in the ever-mellow Puerto Morelos, at the spectacular bird reserve on Isla Contoy, and on lovely, laid-back Isla Mujeres.

Leopard, Xcaret

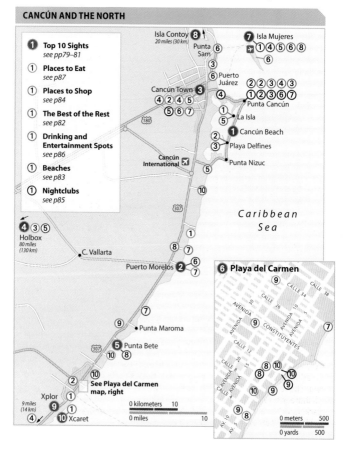

CANCÚN AND THE NORTH

1 Top 10 Sights
   see pp79–81
1 Places to Eat
   see p87
1 Places to Shop
   see p84
1 The Best of the Rest
   see p82
1 Drinking and
   Entertainment Spots
   see p86
1 Beaches
   see p83
1 Nightclubs
   see p85

Isla Contoy 8
20 miles (30 km)
Punta Sam
Puerto Juárez
Cancún Town 3
La Isla
Cancún Beach 1
Playa Delfines
Punta Nizuc
Cancún International
Holbox
80 miles (130 km)
C. Vallarta
Puerto Morelos 2
Punta Maroma
Punta Bete 5
See Playa del Carmen map, right
Xplor
9 miles (14 km)
Xcaret 10

7 Isla Mujeres

Caribbean Sea

0 kilometers 10
0 miles 10

6 **Playa del Carmen**

CALLE 34
CALLE 38
CALLE 26
AVENIDA
CONSTITUYENTES
AVENIDA 10
CALLE 12
AVENIDA 15
AVENIDA
CALLE 20
AV. 10
AV. 5

0 meters 500
0 yards 500

The white-sand arc and azure waters at Cancún Beach

1 Cancún Beach
MAP L4–K6

Every one of the Riviera's beaches has the same wonderful fine white sand, which stays deliciously cool to the touch, but Cancún's is unquestionably the finest, stretching the whole 14 miles (23 km) of Cancún Island. Along it, in the Hotel Zone, are resort hotels, shopping and entertainment centers, water sports and snorkeling, and fun parks, plus the Mayan ruins of El Rey (see pp12–13).

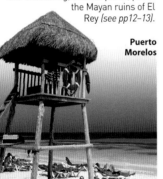

Puerto Morelos

2 Puerto Morelos
MAP R3

This little fishing town was the biggest place on this coast before the rise of Cancún. It has avoided overdevelopment and retains a low-key atmosphere, much loved by the many foreigners who own houses here or stay whole winters in its small hotels. There's a beautiful white beach, and a superb reef close offshore, now protected as a marine park. Local dive operators and fishing guides give individual, friendly service.

3 Cancún Town
MAP J3

On the mainland at the north end of Cancún Island, Ciudad Cancún, also known as "Downtown," was created at the same time as the Hotel Zone in the 1970s. It has developed an atmosphere of its own, though, and the main drag of Avenida Tulum and the nearby squares and avenues are enjoyable places to explore, with plenty of shopping and great restaurants (see pp12–13).

4 Isla Holbox
MAP G1 ■ Passenger ferry from Chiquilá: 8am–7pm daily ■ www.holboxisland.com

This tiny peninsula is fast becoming the Yucatán's hippest destination. Set beside a wide lagoon filled with birds and dolphins, and accessed by a 15-minute ferry journey, Holbox is a wonderfully relaxed village whose sandy streets are lined with small hotels and restaurants. There's a vast beach and, in season, the waters offshore are temporarily home to migrating whale sharks (see p61).

5 Punta Bete
MAP R4

Often unnoticed between Puerto Morelos and Playa del Carmen, and kept off the beaten track by a bumpy 2-mile (3-km) access road through the jungle, this point is flanked by lines of palm-fringed bays – perfect arcs of dazzling white sand by a turquoise sea. They are shared by a few resort hotels, and far more small-scale, cheaper clusters of beach cabañas (see p60 and p83).

Shops at Playa del Carmen

Playa del Carmen
MAP R4

The Riviera's most vibrant street life, by day and night, and its hippest crowds can be found in its fastest-growing resort town. Playa's long-established cool bars and back-packers' haunts mix with modern hotels ranging from big resorts to cozy guesthouses. As well as having wonderful beaches, it's great for diving and snorkeling (see pp16–17).

Isla Mujeres
MAP L1–2

Although it's only a short ferry ride away from Cancún, this 5-mile (8-km) long island, the first place where Spaniards landed in Mexico in 1517, has a very different atmos-phere, with few big hotels, one small

town, a good choice of inexpensive places to stay, and a very easy-going, unhurried beach-village feel. Isla Mujeres is also an excellent diving, snorkeling, and fishing center, with an exciting range of reefs to explore offshore (see pp20–21).

Isla Contoy
MAP H1

Mexico's most important sea-bird reserve covers the whole of this uninhabited island. The terrain is a mix of mangroves, beaches, and coral lagoons that are home to over 50 species of birds – they contain turtle breeding grounds too. Day tours are offered by dive shops on Isla Mujeres (see pp20–21 and p54).

Xplor
MAP Q4 ■ Federal Highway 307, km 282 ■ (998) 251 6560 ■ Open 7am–9pm Mon–Fri (to 8pm week-ends) ■ Adm ■ www.xplor.travel

A trip to Xplor is the ideal day out, which all the family can enjoy. Seven different

Isla Mujeres beachfront

circuits await, including 14 ziplines; two 3-mile (5-km) long amphibious vehicle paths, running along jungle tracks, over rope bridges and through caves; two underground river-raft circuits; and the chance to swim along a subterranean river amongst amazing rock formations (see pp56–7).

River-rafting in Xplor

⑩ Xcaret
MAP Q4

The largest of the Riviera's growing number of eco-parks, just south of Playa del Carmen, this provides a wonderful introduction to the tropical environment of the Yucatán and a full day's worth of things to do – from snorkeling and swimming with dolphins to eye-popping animal and butterfly collections (see pp18–19).

CANCÚN TO TULUM

▶ DAY ONE

Begin by exploring the more traditional side of Cancún with a *desayuno* at one of the **Mercado 28 restaurants** (see p87), in the town market. Then rent a car and drive south through the Hotel Zone along Boulevard Kukulcán.

Call in at the fascinating **Museo Maya** (see p12) and the atmospheric **El Rey** site (see p82). Stop off at **Playa Delfines** (see p83), for crashing surf and a spectacular view back along Cancún Island.

Pause at **Puerto Moreles** (see p79) for a lunch of seafood *ceviche* and a cool beer at **Los Pelícanos** (see p70 and p87), watching the pelicans hang in the breeze. After snorkeling over Puerto's reef, continue on to **Playa del Carmen**. Check out the beach and the shops on Quinta Avenida. As darkness falls, join the strolling crowds along the Quinta.

DAY TWO

After breakfast, continue south towards **Tulum** (see p22–3). Your route will take you past **Xplor** and **Xcaret**, as well as the glamorous vacation spot of **Puerto Aventuras** (see p91), and the gorgeous beaches of **Xpu-Ha** (see p93) and **Akumal** (see p92). In Akumal, have lunch at **Tequilaville** (see p99). On arrival in Tulum, take time to explore the cliff-top Mayan site, then spend the rest of the day swimming and sunbathing on the beach, before enjoying dinner cooked over at open fire at **Hartwood** (see p99).

See map on p78

The Best of the Rest

1 Playacar
MAP Q4

The plusher side of Playa del Carmen, with a fascinating jungle aviary in the midst of landscaped avenues lined with big resort hotels and private villas (see p62).

2 El Rey Site, Cancún
MAP K5 ▪ Open 8am–5pm daily ▪ Adm

This was a relatively small Mayan city, but its layout, with a clearly visible "main street," makes it easy to imagine people bustling about, buying and selling.

The atmospheric El Rey Site

3 El Meco Site, Cancún
MAP K2 ▪ Open 8am–5pm daily ▪ Adm

The remains of an important Mayan city, were probably founded here in about AD 300. They feature impressive carvings of animals and monsters.

4 Cenote Kantun-Chi
MAP P5 ▪ www.kantunchi.com ▪ Open 9am–5pm daily ▪ Adm

Visitors can enjoy a revitalizing swim in the cenote's clear, freshwater pool. There is also a beautiful underground cavern to explore (see p56).

5 Wet'n Wild, Cancún
MAP J6 ▪ Blvd Kukulcán, km 25 ▪ (998) 193 2000 ▪ Open 10am–5pm daily ▪ Adm

With an interactive dolphin pool and a 350- yd (320- m) lazy river, as well as a Wet'n Wild water park, this is the Riviera's biggest fun park (see p56).

6 Puerto Juárez and Punta Sam
MAP K1–2

The little passenger (Puerto Juárez) and car (Punta Sam) ferry ports for Isla Mujeres (see pp20–21) are older than any other part of Cancún.

7 Acamaya
MAP R3

A secluded spot to get away from just about everything, set at the end of the bumpy beach road north from Puerto Morelos. There's a small cabaña hotel and a camping site.

8 Crococún Crocodile Park
MAP R3 ▪ Highway 307, km 31 ▪ (998) 850 3719 ▪ Open 9am–5pm daily ▪ Adm

Crocodiles are the key attraction, but monkeys and parrots, along with stranger elements of the local wildlife, are also a draw (see p64).

9 Punta Maroma
MAP R4

Among the palm-fringed bays at Punta Maroma are several reserved exclusively for guests at the luxurious Maroma retreat (see p128).

10 Moon Palace
MAP R3 ▪ (998) 881 6000 or (877) 325 1531 ▪ www.palace resorts.com

One of the largest and best equipped of the Riviera's resort complexes, set in its own area of jungle to the south of Cancún (see p128).

Moon Palace resort complex

Beaches

Visitors enjoying the waters off the popular Playa Norte beach, Isla Mujeres

1 Playa Norte, Isla Mujeres
MAP L1

The beach bums' favorite on Isla, this compact strip of white sand has plenty to keep you entertained, from pedalos, kayaks, and snorkeling to great bars under the palms.

2 Playa Gaviotas, Cancún
MAP L4 ■ Blvd Kukulcán, km 9

One of the best beaches on the east side of Cancún, and located in the partying center, Playa Gaviotas is the perfect place for after-party relaxation. Adjacent is the City Beach Club.

3 Playa Delfines, Cancún
MAP K5 ■ Blvd Kukulcán, km 18

A great place to find space to stretch out, with huge banks of white sand above pounding ocean surf. There's an amazing view north along the beachscape of Cancún Island.

4 Playa Secreto, Isla Mujeres
MAP L1

This broad, sheltered, shallow inlet tucked away from the main North Beach is especially good for small kids. Its waters are always tranquil, and the beach is rarely crowded.

5 Isla Holbox
MAP G1

For lovers of real seclusion, with miles of beach from which to pick a spot that's just right. The island faces the opal waters of the Gulf of Mexico, however, so there's no coral (see p79).

6 Puerto Morelos
MAP R3

Excellent for carefree swimming, Puerto Morelos boasts not only fine, uncrowded white sands, but also a reef full of vivid underwater life just offshore (see p79).

7 Playa del Secreto
MAP R4

A short way south of Puerto Morelos, this big, broad, white-sand beach is mostly fronted by private villas, with scarcely any hotels, so there's never any shortage of space.

8 Punta Bete
MAP R4

One of the most beautiful spots on the whole Riviera – palms, white-sand bays, and turquoise sea. A terrible access road helps keep it that way (see p79).

9 Playa del Carmen
MAP Q4

Playa's main town beach is the place to go to survey other sun worshippers, and to showcase your skills at beach volleyball and other seaside pursuits (see pp16–17).

10 Chunzubul, Playa del Carmen
MAP Q4

Keep walking along the beach north from Playa to find endless space, the best snorkeling and diving spots, and nudist beaches. It is safest to avoid leaving bags unattended in the really quiet spots (see pp120–21).

See map on p78

Places to Shop

1 La Casa del Arte Mexicano, Cancún

MAP K3 ▪ Blvd Kukulcán, km 4

The gift shop at this folk-art museum, in the grounds of Xcaret, stocks high-quality crafts from all over Mexico, including some fun toys.

2 Forum by the Sea, Cancún

MAP K4 ▪ Blvd Kukulcán, km 9.5
▪ Open 10am–midnight daily

Highlights here are perfume and jewelry stores and brands such as Harley Davidson and Zingara. It also has a huge Hard Rock at its center.

3 Coral Negro, Cancún

MAP L4 ▪ Boulevard Kukulcán, km 9.5

A rambling jewelry and handicrafts bazaar a few steps from the Forum. You can find fine traditional craft-work here, as well as a lot of junk.

4 Plaza Caracol, Cancún

MAP K4 ▪ Blvd Kukulcán, km 8.5

One of the biggest and most varied of the Cancún malls, with engaging toy shops, beachwear, fine jewelry, and a huge choice of restaurants in an attractive, light-filled building.

5 La Isla, Cancún

MAP K4 ▪ Blvd Kukulcán, km 12.5

One of the most stylish of the Hotel Zone's malls, built as an artificial island surrounded by Venetian-style "canals." It's the place for top names such as Coach, Diesel and Zara.

6 Mercado 23, Cancún

MAP J3 ▪ Off Avenida Tulum, on Calle Cedro

This colorful little open-air market is where locals go to shop for meat, vegetables, herbal cures, and even party supplies and piñatas.

7 Mercado 28, Cancún

MAP J3 ▪ Av Xel-Ha and Av Tankah

The town market offers old-style shopping – stands of *huarache* sandals and panama hats, and tables full of fresh vegetables and fruit – plus a great food court (see p87).

8 Avenida Hidalgo, Isla Mujeres Town

MAP L1

This is Isla's main street, and its main drag for leisurely browsing. Here and in parallel Av Juárez small shops offer painted wooden birds, and local shell and coral jewelry.

9 Super Telas, Playa del Carmen

MAP Q4 ▪ Constituyentes, Plaza Las Perlas

Fine quality Mexican textiles (*telas*), in traditional or original designs, can be found in this original shop.

10 Caracol, Playa del Carmen

MAP Q4 ▪ Av 5, from Calle 6 to 84

The specialties at this two-story boutique are textiles and embroidery from all over Mexico – particularly Chiapas – and from Guatemala.

The canalside stores of La Isla, Cancún

Nightclubs

1 Coco Bongo, Cancún
MAP L4 ▪ Blvd Kukulcán, km 9.5 ▪ (998) 883 5061 ▪ Open from 10:30pm daily ▪ Adm

Cancún's most high-powered, high-tech, multilevel mega-club, with a wide-ranging menu of music options (see p67).

A gig by the Bingo Players, Palazzo

2 Palazzo, Cancún
MAP L4 ▪ Blvd Kukulcán, km 9 ▪ (998) 848 8380 ▪ Open from 10pm daily ▪ Adm

Big on audio and lighting systems (glitz is the byword here), Palazzo offers live gigs by well-known acts.

3 Dady'O, Cancún
MAP L4 ▪ Blvd Kukulcán, km 9.5 ▪ (998) 883 3333 ▪ Dady'O open from 10pm daily, Sweet open from 6pm daily ▪ Adm

The college crowd's favorite holds bikini nights and other rowdy fun. Sweet, next door, often hosts live bands (see p67).

4 Captain Hook's Pirate Night, Cancún
MAP K3 ▪ El Embarcadero, Blvd Kukulcán, km 4.5 ▪ Check in 6:30pm daily ▪ Adm

Dinner cruises are normally more sedate than clubbing in Cancún, but Captain Hook's, with its "pirate crew," is still pretty boisterous (see p66).

5 Grand Mambo Café, Cancún
MAP H3 ▪ Plaza Hong Kong local 31 ▪ (998) 844 4536 ▪ Open from 10:30pm Wed–Sat

The best place to let your hair down in Cancún, Grand Mambo Café features bands from Central and Southern America, and the Caribbean.

6 Cun Crawl, Cancún
MAP L4 ▪ Blvd Kukulcán, km 9.5 ▪ (998) 165 0699

Chill out in the lounge area, or hit the dance floor, as the DJs mix and play creative blends of European music at this chic nightclub.

7 The City, Cancún
MAP L4 ▪ Blvd Kukulcán, km 9.5 ▪ (998) 848 8385 (ext 115) ▪ Nightclub open from 10pm daily ▪ Casual dress but no sandals or bathing suits ▪ Adm

This huge, modern nightclub also includes a beach club, restaurant, bar, and lounge.

8 La Santanera, Playa del Carmen
MAP Q4 ▪ Calle 4, between Av 5 and Av 12 ▪ (984) 803 2856 ▪ Open from 11pm daily ▪ Adm

A two-story club offering two venues in one. Each night DJs play electronica and house music (see p66).

9 Blue Parrot Beach Club, Playa del Carmen
MAP Q4 ▪ Calle 12 Norte ▪ (984) 879 4749 ▪ Open from 11pm daily ▪ Adm

Dance under the stars at this beachfront club. DJs perform nightly.

10 La Vaquita, Playa del Carmen
MAP Q4 ▪ Calle 12 Norte ▪ (998) 848 8380 ▪ Open 11pm–6am daily ▪ Adm

This lively nightclub, whose name means "Little Cow," is anything but pastoral, and has a man dressed as a cow, offering shots to the crowds.

See map on p78

Drinking and Entertainment Spots

1 La Madonna, Cancún
MAP K4 ▪ La Isla, Blvd Kukulcán, km 12.5 ▪ $$

An elegant bar-restaurant in the La Isla mall, with decor that's a hybrid of Baroque and Art Nouveau.

The quirky cave setting of Alux

2 Alux, Playa del Carmen
MAP Q4 ▪ Av Juaréz 217 ▪ $$

This restaurant-bar has the most unusual setting in Playa: an atmospheric cave. It is a good spot for an evening drink or dinner, though prices are a little high. Later in the night, dance to DJs or live jazz.

3 Señor Frog's, Cancún
MAP L4 ▪ Blvd Kukulcán, km 9.5 ▪ $

Beside Laguna Nichupté, this is one of the most popular Cancún outlets of the Anderson group (see p66). Party atmosphere, often with rock bands, guaranteed.

4 El Pabilo, Cancún
MAP J3 ▪ Av Yaxchilán 31 ▪ $

This cozy café, with a Bohemian feel, offers a welcome respite from loud nightclubs. Live music by local musicians and Cuban expats on weekends.

5 Buho's, Isla Mujeres
MAP L1 ▪ Playa Norte ▪ $

Isla's funkiest beach bar has a palm roof to give shade, and is right on the sand, just steps away from the sea. It offers Mexican snacks to go with the cocktails and chilled beers.

6 El Café Cito, Isla Mujeres
MAP L1 ▪ Av Juárez, corner of Av Matamoros, Isla Town ▪ $

This mellow place, a few streets from the beach, offers excellent breakfasts and superior coffee, and fresh juice combos later in the day.

7 Mamita's Beach Club, Playa del Carmen
MAP Q4 ▪ Beach at Calle 28 ▪ $

One of the nicest beaches in Playa is also the most popular daytime party spot, with loungers and hammocks for rent alongside the usual chairs, a DJ, and strong Margaritas.

8 Deseo Lounge, Playa del Carmen
MAP Q4 ▪ Deseo Hotel, Av 5, by Calle 12 ▪ $$

A spectacular chrome-and-glass bar that wouldn't be out of place in New York or Miami Beach. Luminous house cocktails are the specialty.

9 Pez Vela, Playa del Carmen
MAP Q4 ▪ Av 5, by Calle 2 ▪ $

Ever popular bar-restaurant with a huge outside terrace that's a fixture on the Quinta Avenida promenade. The style is hippy-Caribbean, helped along by reggae and rock bands.

10 Diablito Cha Cha Cha, Playa del Carmen
MAP Q4 ▪ Calle 12 at Av 1 Norte ▪ $

With comfortable sofas and a stylish clientele, this is the place to warm up before hitting the bigger dance clubs (see p67).

Places to Eat

PRICE CATEGORIES

For a three-course meal for one with a beer or soda (or equivalent meal), taxes and extra charges.

....

$ under $15 $$ $15–$35 $$$ over $35

1 **Le Chique, Cancún**
MAP R3 ■ Puerto Morelos km 27.5 ■ (998) 872 8450 ■ $$$

With classic dishes, such as *cochinita pibil (see p68),* appealing to the palate and the eye, Le Chique is a perfect place to celebrate special occasions.

2 **La Habichuela, Cancún**
MAP J3 ■ Calle Margaritas 25 ■ (998) 840 6240 ■ $$$

A charming specialist in Yucatecan and Mexican tropical seafood in a softly lit garden by the tranquil Parque de las Palapas *(see p70).*

3 **El Chapulim, Isla Holbox**
MAP G1 ■ Av Tiburón Ballena ■ $$

Don't let the lack of a menu deter you from trying out this bistro, which has the best fresh seafood in town and over 25 varieties of Mexican beer.

4 **La Parrilla, Cancún**
MAP J3 ■ Av Yaxchilán 51 ■ (998) 193 3973 ■ $$

With daily mariachi music creating a warm atmosphere, La Parrilla offers a good range of Mexican favorites such as grilled meats, soups, and fondues *(see p70).*

La Parrilla, Cancún

5 **Mercado 28 Restaurants, Cancún**
MAP J3 ■ Av Xel-Ha and Av Tankah ■ No credit cards ■ $

The courtyard of the town market is packed with canopied tables spilling out from restaurants. The traditional food served, such as *pollo con mole (see p68),* is fun and cheap.

6 **Da Luisa, Isla Mujeres**
MAP L1 ■ Av Jesús Martinez s/n ■ (998) 888 0107 ■ $$

Enjoy Caribbean-Mediterranean fusion cuisine (fresh seafood, pork, or chicken) with skyline views at this quiet, romantic restaurant.

7 **Los Pelícanos, Puerto Morelos**
MAP R3 ■ On the Plaza ■ $$

Linger over the renowned seafood cocktails or one of the subtle fish dishes at one of the all-time best beach-terrace restaurants *(see p70).*

8 **La Casa del Agua, Playa del Carmen**
MAP Q4 ■ Av 5, by Calle 2 ■ (984) 803 0232 ■ $$$

This stylish café-restaurant-gallery surveys the Quinta Avenida bustle from an airy balcony. The menu features an imaginative, Mexican-European mix.

9 **Los Aguachiles, Playa del Carmen**
MAP Q4 ■ Corner of Calle 34 and Av 25 ■ $

A low-key open-air snack joint, this place offers an array of delicious tacos and tostadas and an even larger selection of salsas and condiments with which to personalize them

10 **Las Brisas, Playa del Carmen**
MAP Q4 ■ Carretera Federal Cancún–Playa del Carmen ■ $$$

This big terrace-restaurant has a simple style, but its fresh local seafood is some of the best in town.

See map on p78

📻 Cozumel and the South

The southern stretch of the Riviera is the less publicized, less built-up part of this coast, but it still offers the choice between luxury resorts and out-of-the-way places – except that here the resorts are not so hectic, and the untouched corners are more remote. Offshore, Cozumel is a super-relaxing island that offers fabulous diving opportunities. Onshore are some of the Caribbean's most dazzling tropical beaches, such as the seven bays of Xpu-Ha and the crescent of Media Luna Bay. They lead down the coast to the great beach refuge of Tulum, with its Mayan temple sites. A little way inland is another massive Mayan site, the forest-clad city of Cobá.

Sombrero

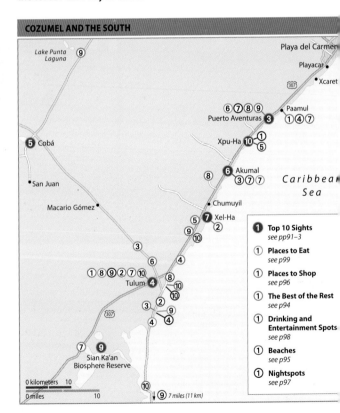

COZUMEL AND THE SOUTH

Lake Punta Laguna ⑨

Playa del Carmen

Playacar

Xcaret

307

⑥⑦⑧⑨ Puerto Aventuras ❸ • Paamul ①④⑦

Xpu-Ha ⑩ ①⑤

❺ Cobá

Akumal
⑧ ❻ ③⑦⑦

Caribbean Sea

• San Juan

Macario Gómez •

• Chumuyil

⑤ ❼ Xel-Ha
②
⑨ ⑩

③

⑥ ④
①⑧⑨②⑦⑩ ⑧
Tulum ❹ ⑩
⑩
③ ② ⑨
307 ④ ④

⑦ ⑨
Sian Ka'an Biosphere Reserve

	Top 10 Sights see pp91–3
①	Places to Eat see p99
①	Places to Shop see p96
①	The Best of the Rest see p94
①	Drinking and Entertainment Spots see p98
①	Beaches see p95
①	Nightspots see p97

0 kilometers 10
0 miles 10

⑩
↓⑨ 7 miles (11 km)

Previous pages Horse-drawn carriage in front of the monastery of San Antonio in Izamal

Cozumel
MAP R5

Gleaming jewelry stores along the waterfront in San Miguel combine with an easy-going, small-town charm that has long made this island a favorite with families. It's a great place to settle into at a leisurely pace, maybe going diving one day, then exploring a little the next: around the island are Mayan sites, windblown cliffs, a fascinating natural wildlife park at Punta Sur, and lovely beaches and snorkeling spots on the west coast (see pp14–15).

San Gervasio, Cozumel
MAP R5 ▪ (998) 849 2885
▪ Open 8am–4pm daily ▪ Adm

The remains of the Mayan capital of Cozumel, conquered by Cortés and his Spanish soldiers in 1519, are in the middle of the island. Its buildings are small compared to those of the great Mayan cities, but there are many of them – and discovering them, through woods full of wonderful scents, flowers, and exotic birds, involves a lovely walk (see p15).

Puerto Aventuras
MAP Q5

Puerto Aventuras is the biggest, most opulent resort on the southern Riviera, a specially created vacation village around an inlet that's now a pretty pleasure port lined with shops and restaurants. The nine-hole golf course is attractive, and the marina is the best-equipped on the whole Riviera, making it a popular base for serious deep-sea fishing enthusiasts. In another part of the harbor you can swim with dolphins (see p21).

The clifftop ruins at Tulum

Tulum
MAP P6

Home to a ruined Mayan city perched up on a clifftop, a 7-mile (11-km) palm-fringed beach, and an array of inventive restaurants and boutique hotels, Tulum is one of the region's most attractive destinations, particularly popular with independent travelers looking for a quieter spot than Playa or Cancún. There's good fishing and diving offshore, and the area around is dotted with beautiful cenotes to explore (see pp58–9).

Visitors at the pyramid at Cobá

6 Akumal
MAP P5

Long a favorite dive destination, with fabulous reefs and places for cave diving, Akumal has grown a good deal without being overwhelmed. It spreads over several long, lovely bays – Media Luna is the most beautiful, with the delightful Yal-Ku lagoon (see p65). There are more apartments, villas, and small hotels than big developments. The beaches near Akumal village are favorite turtle breeding grounds.

7 Xel-Ha
MAP P6 ■ (998) 251 6560 ■ Open 8:30am–7pm daily ■ Adm ■ www.xelha.com

One of the most luxuriant coral inlets on the coast has been made into a "snorkel park" that's one of the Riviera's most popular attractions – experienced divers may find it tame, but the easy snorkeling is great for families. Around it is a forest park and a beach. Just outside the park and across the highway is the Mayan site of Xel-Ha (see p94).

5 Cobá
MAP M5 ■ Open 8am–5pm daily ■ Adm ■ www.inah.gob.mx

This huge Mayan city – once home to around 50,000 people – was the great rival of Chichén Itzá. It's a very different place to visit – it's spread out around several large lakes, and to find its massive buildings you follow fascinating walks through thick forest full of birds. Yucatán's tallest pyramid is here (see p45).

8 The Cozumel Reefs
Cozumel's greatest glory is its 20-plus coral reefs, an awe-inspiring undersea world of caves, canyons, and

A variety of sealife amid the vibrant coral at the Cozumel Reefs

coral "forests" teeming with life, from sea cucumbers and brilliantly luminous angelfish to graceful rays and the occasional shark. The water is almost perfectly clear and Chankanaab and Paraíso reefs are close inshore, so can be appreciated even by inexperienced divers and snorkelers (see p15).

THE SACBÉ OF COBÁ

Cobá was the center of the largest network of sacbé (or "white ways"), Mayan raised stone-paved roads, in the Mayan world. They connected the various parts of the city, as well as linked it to vassal-cities. About AD 800 Cobá built the longest ever sacbé, of over 60 miles (100 km), to Yaxuná in the west, to help reinforce it in wars with Chichén – unsuccessfully, as Cobá was defeated shortly afterward.

9 Sian Ka'an Biosphere Reserve

MAP F5–6

Mexico's largest wetland nature reserve, and a UNESCO World Heritage Site, Sian Ka'an brings the Riviera to an end just south of Tulum. Its vast area of virtually untouched mangroves, jungle, and beaches contains an extraordinary range of birds and wildlife, and the one-day tours run by local organizations give a glimpse of the intricate, constantly surprising interplay of nature in this rare environment. The few inhabited spots along the coast are wonderful for fishing, and have a feel of tranquil isolation (see pp26–7).

10 Xpu-Ha

MAP P5

All along these seven gracefully sweeping bays, 2 miles (3 km) south of Puerto Aventuras, are some of the Riviera's most idyllic beaches, with exuberantly alive reefs and some of the most exquisite turquoise waters. Several are now occupied by resort complexes. However, two (signposted X-4 and X-7 from the highway) are still open to anyone, and at X-7 there are some small cabañas, a camping site, and a dive shop.

COZUMEL IN A DAY

▶ MORNING

Start with breakfast, coffee, or a drink at Las Palmeras (see p98), watching the new arrivals off the Playa del Carmen ferry. Browse in the jewelry and souvenir shops along the waterfront and in the streets around the square, but don't buy anything yet. Rent a car and head out of town down Avenida Juárez to the Mayan site of **San Gervasio** (see p91). If you hire the services of a guide at the entrance, don't let them hurry you, but take time to notice the birds and vegetation as much of an attraction as the ruins. Back at the main road, head left to meet the east coast at windswept **Punta Santa Cecilia** (see p14). Turn south down the road beside the rocks and waves for a lunch of mixed fish and seafood on the beach at Chen Río (see p99).

AFTERNOON

Carry on down the coast to **Punta Sur Eco Beach Park**. From the parking lot, walk down to Punta Celaraín lighthouse and the strange little Mayan temple called the Caracol, and follow the nature trail to try and see some crocodiles and flamingos.

You can snorkel at Punta Sur, but you'll see more underwater life if you carry on to **Laguna Chankanaab**. If all you want is a placid beach, call in at **Playa San Francisco** (see p95). Drive back to town, and don't miss the sunset from the waterfront Malecón. Take another look at the shops, and buy anything you may have spotted on your morning walk.

See map on pp90–91 ←

The Best of the Rest

 Paamul
MAP Q5

The favorite destination for RV travelers, who take advantage of generous long-term rates to settle in for the whole winter. The camp site also has cabañas (see p129), a beach bar (p95), and a dive shop.

 Xel-Ha Ruins
MAP P6 ▪ Open 8:30am–7pm daily ▪ Adm

Across the highway from the popular snorkel park, this ruined Mayan city is one of the oldest in the region. On some buildings there are murals dating back to about AD 200.

 Aktun-Ha Cenote/ Car Wash
MAP N6

Another fine swimming-hole cenote set amid rocks and woods toward Cobá. Snorkelers can explore the huge main cavern; divers (with guides) can go further.

Visitors inside the Aktun-Ha Cenote

 Tankah
MAP P6

Off the beaten track, Tankah is a placid, narrow beach with a fine reef, a restaurant, and a small cluster of villas and hotels. Behind the beach, by the Casa Cenote restaurant, there's a broad, reed-lined cenote, so it's a toss-up between swimming in the surf or the freshwater pool.

 Dos Ojos Cenote
MAP P6

Dos Ojos is very possibly the world's longest underwater cave system. The snorkeling or diving tours run by the diving tour operators are a memorable experience (see p51).

 Gran Cenote
MAP N6

The Cobá road north from Tulum is one of the best places to find swim-mable cenotes, and this is one of the most beautiful, a crystal-clear pool that's a must-try for swimmers and snorkelers (see p59).

 Muyil Site
MAP G4 ▪ Open 8am–5pm daily ▪ Adm

The location is the attraction of this old, atmospheric Mayan city set in hot, steamy jungle between the Highway and Lake Chunyaxché, in the Sian Ka'an reserve.

 Aktun-Chen Cave
MAP P5

This giant cave in thick jungle in a nature park has an awesome series of chambers and stalagmite towers, plus an underground river (see p57).

 Punta Laguna
MAP N4

Set in a tiny village by a forest lake north of Cobá, this nature reserve is one of the best places to see spider monkeys in the Yucatán. Villagers will act as guides (see p54).

10 Road from Boca Paila to Punta Allen
MAP G4–5

Good for the adventurous, this is one of the bumpiest, rutted, overgrown, and deserted roads in the Yucatán, with great vistas of sea and forest.

Beaches

Enjoying the waters at Playa Sol

1 Playa San Francisco and Playa Sol, Cozumel
MAP R5–6

These are two of the many great beaches on Cozumel's southwest coast: San Francisco and others near it are good for relaxation; Sol is best if you want a beach with lots going on.

2 South Beach, Tulum
MAP P6

The place for people who want to find some seclusion in Tulum, with longer, broader, whiter beaches, acres of space, and quite luxurious comforts in some cabañas.

3 Media Luna Bay, Akumal
MAP P5

"Half Moon Bay" is an exquisite, near-perfect crescent of brilliant white sand and calm sea. The atmosphere is just as tranquil: around it there are condos and villas; at the north end is the lovely Yal-Ku lagoon (see p65).

4 Paamul
MAP Q5

A curving white-sand bay with a beach bar and cabañas (see p129). With over a mile (2 km) of beach, the camp site doesn't obstruct the view, and the sands are never crowded.

5 Xpu-Ha
MAP P5

Seven bays with some of the coolest, whitest sand and most colorful coral on the Riviera. Several are occupied by resorts, but X-4 and X-7 (see p93) are open to anyone.

6 Chen Río, Cozumel
MAP R5

This is the best beach on Cozumel's rugged eastern shore, with a sheltered cove for swimming, with surfing further along. There's a beach restaurant worth a special visit (see p70).

7 Akumal Village
MAP P5

A bustling beach in the center of Akumal; behind it there's a good choice of low-key bars and shops.

8 North Beach, Tulum
MAP P6

The beaches at the north end of Tulum are great if you want to hang out and get to know people in the inexpensive cabañas. They also have the best view of the ruins (see pp22–3).

9 Punta Xamach and Conoco
MAP G5

Getting to these remote, deserted beaches involves negotiating the wild, rutted road between Boca Paila and Punta Allen.

10 Punta Solimán
MAP P6

Shaded by palms, this near-empty beach feels remote, even though it's only down a dirt-track from the highway. A few boats and a bar (see p98) are the main signs of habitation.

Tranquil Punta Solimán

Places to Shop

1 Azul Gallery, Cozumel
MAP R5 ▪ 449 Av 15 Norte, between Calle 8 and Calle 10

Watch artist Greg Dietrich engrave blown glass to create unique vessels and lamps at this quaint art gallery. Paintings, jewelry, and other items made by local artists are also on display.

Engraved glass, Azul Gallery

2 Tulum Bazaar, Tulum
MAP P6 ▪ Av Tulum

An amazing hotchpotch of stores in true Mexican flea-market style. Souvenirs, Mayan handicrafts, textiles, and jewelry abound. Be ready to haggle for the best deals.

3 Josa, Tulum
MAP P6 ▪ (984) 115 8441 ▪ Carretera Boca Paila km 1.5 Quintana Roo, Tulum

Inspired by the tropical and relaxed vibe of the Tulum beaches, this chic boutique sells fashionable accessories and clothing for women.

4 Punta Langosta, Cozumel
MAP R5

This leisure mall set in the cruise terminal has major international fashion names plus upscale handicrafts and glittering gem stores.

5 Los Cinco Soles, Cozumel
MAP R5 ▪ Av Rafael Melgar 27, by Calle 8

This Malecón handicrafts store is the place to do all your souvenir shopping in one go – clothes, tablecloths, jewelry, glassware, metal or papier-mâché birds and animals, and more.

6 Unicornio, Cozumel
MAP R5 ▪ Av 5 Sur, near Calle 1 Sur

A big, varied crafts dealer, with especially good ceramics and painted wood. There's junk as well as quality pieces, but it's a great place to browse.

7 Shalom, Tulum
MAP P6 ▪ Av Tulum, between Calle Orion and Calle Centauro

Get dressed for a Tulum-style beach party at this cool shop selling hippy-style clothing plus sleeker items that you could wear when out clubbing.

8 Pro Dive, Cozumel
MAP R5 ▪ Av Adolfo Rosado Salas 198, corner of Av 5

First port of call for self-sufficient sea-explorers, with every possible kind of diving and snorkeling gear.

9 Puerto Aventuras
MAP Q5

A small, stylish group of shops. Among the cigars and sophisticated jewelry, you'll also find Mexican designer clothing at Arte Maya and fine handicrafts at El Guerrero.

10 Mixik Artesanías, Tulum
MAP P6 ▪ Av Tulum, opposite the bus terminal

This little store has a high-quality collection of colorful craftwork from every part of the country.

Punta Langosta, Cozumel

Nightspots

1 Al Cielo, Puerto Aventuras
MAP Q5 ■ Xpu-Ha Beach ■ Open 11:30am–9pm daily ■ Adm

The exclusive Al Cielo offers guests one-of-a-kind events on Xpu-Ha Beach, often with the moonlit ocean as a backdrop. It features top-class musicians, dancers, and other entertainment.

2 La Internacional Cervecería, Cozumel
MAP R5 ■ (987) 869 1289 ■ Av Rafael Melgar, by 7 Sur and 11 Sur

With a focus on beers, this bar offers a fine selection of international and Mexican brews, specially sourced from craft brewers around the country.

3 Plaza del Sol, Cozumel
MAP R5 ■ Av Melgar at Av Juárez

Cozumel doesn't have a particularly wild nightlife. Instead, San Miguel's central plaza is the best place to be – especially on Sundays, when there's usually live music.

4 La Zebra, Tulum
MAP G4 ■ Beach road, km 4.6

La Zebra's Sunday night salsa party draws people from up and down the beach as well as from town. Come early for free dance classes.

5 Hard Rock Café, Cozumel
MAP R5 ■ Av Rafael Melgar 2A ■ Open from 10pm daily ■ Adm

The Mayan-style architecture of the building makes this a stunning location for the rock memorabilia chain. Occasional live music.

6 Jimmy Buffett's Margaritaville, Cozumel
MAP R5 ■ Av Rafael Melgar 799, Col Centro ■ Open 9am–11pm Mon–Sat

On the water, with great views and familiar fare, this branch of the chain is a huge hit with visitors.

7 Joel's Bar, Puerto Aventuras
MAP Q5 ■ On the Marina ■ Open 4pm–1am daily

Joel's Bar offers a wide range of entertainment, including dolphin shows and live music, preceded or accompanied by dinner.

Carlos'n Charlie's, Cozumel

8 Carlos'n Charlie's, Cozumel
MAP R5 ■ Av Rafael Melgar 551 ■ Open from 11am daily

Cozumel's biggest bar, restaurant, and music venue is the place where you're assured of finding a (usually pretty raucous) crowd every night, partying in the open air to classic rock circa 1970 to present (see p67).

9 Batey Mojito and Guarapo Bar, Tulum
MAP P6 ■ Calle Centauro Sur by Av Tulum and Andromeda Oriente

The main late-night hangout in the town of Tulum, featuring live bands and innovative drinks. Their mojitos, with freshly cut cane juice and rum, are a big hit.

10 Mezzanine, Tulum
MAP P6 ■ Carretera Boca Paila km 1.5 ■ Open from 11am daily ■ No credit cards ■ Adm

This stylish restaurant-bar combines luxurious indulgence with eco-friendly policies. Enjoy one of their cocktails while chilling to the sounds of guest DJs.

See map on pp90–91

Drinking and Entertainment Spots

1 Teetotum
MAP P6 ▪ $$

Attached to the hotel of the same name, on the road between Tulum town and the beach. The cocktail list – try the "Mayan Elder": mezcal, angostura bitters, orange, and cherry juice – and laid-back vibe make it a cool spot for an evening drink.

Las Palmeras, Cozumel

2 Las Palmeras, Cozumel
MAP R5 ▪ Av Rafael Melgar–Plaza Cozumel ▪ $$

A big, friendly, Caribbean hut of a bar, opposite the ferry landing on San Miguel's main plaza. As well as being great for drinks, it does highly enjoyable breakfasts.

3 Kelley's, Cozumel
MAP R5 ▪ Av 10, between Av Salas and Calle 1 ▪ $

Popular with divers and tours, this outdoor bar can get rowdy when an American football game is on. It's the ideal spot for a beer and a burger.

4 Viva México, Cozumel
MAP R5 ▪ Av Rafael E. Melgar ▪ $

This is one of the few cafés with a sea view in San Miguel, serving margaritas, mojitos, and daiquiris, and classic Mexican and American food.

5 Café del Museo, Cozumel
MAP R5 ▪ Av Rafael Melgar, by Calle 4 ▪ Open 9am–5pm daily ▪ $

This very relaxing, pretty café on the roof of Cozumel's museum *(see p14)* has a great view of the waterfront and good coffee. It does tasty breakfasts and snacks too.

6 Mezcalito's, Cozumel
MAP R5 ▪ Punta Santa Cecilia ▪ $$

An old favorite, this laid-back beach restaurant is set in a wonderful location, where the cross-island road meets the east coast. Enjoy a soundtrack of crashing surf.

7 Cabañas Paamul
MAP Q5 ▪ $

Deep shade and an ideal view over the beach make the bar in the Paamul cabañas and camping site *(see p129)* a great place to recharge after time in the sun. Snacks are also available.

8 Piña Colada, Puerto Aventuras
MAP Q5 ▪ $$

Puerto Aventuras' favorite beach bar has a big *palapa* roof. Elaborate tropical cocktails are the specialty.

9 Oscar y Lalo, Punta Solimán
MAP P6 ▪ $

Punta Solimán has a desert-island feel, and so does its only bar. Oscar and Lalo, who also run the camping site and rent kayaks, are friendly and cook great fresh seafood.

10 El Paraíso, Tulum
MAP P6 ▪ Beach road km 5.5 ▪ $

Many of Tulum's cabaña-clusters have bars, but Paraíso, near the ruins, has the best view, with a big terrace for catching the breeze.

Places to Eat

PRICE CATEGORIES

For a three-course meal for one with a beer or soda (or equivalent meal), taxes, and extra charges.

$ under $15 $$ $15–$35 $$$ over $35

1 Guido's, Cozumel
MAP R5 ■ Av Melgar 23, between Calle 6 and Calle 8 ■ (987) 872 0946 ■ $$$

It is best known for its rich lasagne, but Guido's other Italian food, including wood-oven pizzas, is great too. Enjoy it all outside in the garden.

2 Rock'n Java, Cozumel
MAP R5 ■ Av Rafael Melgar 602, between Calle 7 and Av Quintana Roo ■ (987) 872 4405 ■ $$

The big fresh salads and sandwiches are great at this American-run café on the water. Save some room for a huge slice of apple pie or one of the other gooey desserts.

Casa Denis, Cozumel

3 Casa Denis, Cozumel
MAP R5 ■ Calle 1 Sur, by Av 5 ■ from 7am daily ■ No credit cards ■ $$

One of the island's oldest venues, Casa Denis serves classic Yucatecan dishes (see pp68–9) at low prices.

4 Hechizo
MAP P6 ■ Rancho San Eric, Tulum Beach Rd, km 7.5 ■ $$$

A romantic spot for dinner, with only a handful of tables set in a tranquil location. There's no menu: the chef, who worked for the Ritz-Carlton in Singapore, cooks a different nightly choice, based on what is in season.

5 La Cocay, Cozumel
MAP R5 ■ Calle 8, between Av 10 and Av 15 ■ $$$

Set in a Caribbean-style wooden hut, this mellow place offers a range of Mediterranean-inspired dishes.

6 Ristorante Massimo, Puerto Aventuras
MAP Q5 ■ Plaza Marina ■ (984) 873 5418 ■ $$

This restaurant is located in a cabaña with a sea view. The menu offers a variety of classic American and Italian dishes.

7 Tequilaville, Akumal
MAP P5 ■ Calle Principal ■ (984) 875 9022 ■ $$

This small eatery serves a pleasant selection of authentic Mexican food and, allegedly, the best hamburger in the Riviera Maya.

8 Cetli, Tulum
MAP P6 ■ Calle Polar at Calle Orion ■ (984) 108 0681 ■ $$

A Mexico City-trained chef-owner turns out light, refined versions of Mexican classics such as *chiles en nogada* (stuffed chilies with walnut sauce) at this casual eatery.

9 Hartwood, Tulum
MAP P6 ■ Tulum Beach Rd, km 7.6 ■ $$$

Across from the beach and set in lush jungle, Hartwood's chefs cook over an open fire and produce top-class cuisine. You'll probably have to queue, but it is worth the wait.

10 Chen Río, Cozumel
MAP R5 ■ Chen Río Beach ■ No credit cards ■ $$

The best restaurant on Cozumel's east coast, and a wonderful place to eat on the beach.

See map on pp90–91

🔟 The Central Heartland

An unmistakable Yucatecan identity and sense of their own culture distinguishes towns such as Valladolid or Tizimín, with Spanish colonial churches and squares, Mayan women selling luscious fruit and colorful flowers, and a gently paced street life. The ancestors of the modern Maya built some of their greatest creations here, at Ek-Balam and the city of Chichén Itzá. Giant underground caverns and magical cenote pools lie beneath the landscape.

Brown pelican

1 Balankanché Caves
MAP E3 ■ Open 8am–5pm daily ■ Adm

This great labyrinthine complex of caves extends for miles under the Yucatán forest. Caves were sacred for the ancient Maya and, in one spectacular chamber, the sanctuary, remains were found of over 100 ritual incense burners. The compulsory tour ends in a magical chamber with a perfectly still pool, in which the cave bottom seen through the water is a mirror image of the roof.

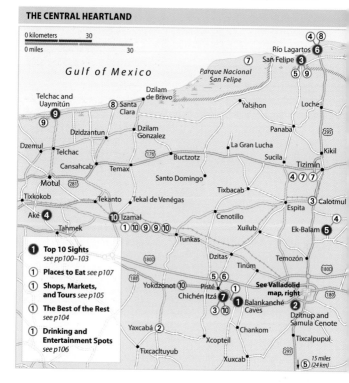

THE CENTRAL HEARTLAND

Top 10 Sights
see pp100–103

Places to Eat see p107

Shops, Markets, and Tours see p105

The Best of the Rest see p104

Drinking and Entertainment Spots see p106

The huge cavern of Dzitnup Cenote

2 Dzitnup and Samula Cenote

MAP E3 ▪ Dzitnup village ▪ Open 8am–5pm daily ▪ Adm

Easily accessible from Valladolid, these two spectacular swimmable cenotes are among the great sights of the Yucatán. Dzitnup is entered through a cramped tunnel, which emerges into a vast, cathedral-like cavern, pierced by a shaft of sunlight and filled with tower-shaped rocks. A five-minute walk away, Samula is a large, shallow pool of crystal-clear water, into which the roots of an aged tree dangle through a crack in the rocky ceiling (see p58).

3 San Felipe

MAP E1

West of Río Lagartos, this village is smaller and has a superb, usually near-empty beach on the sandbar across the lagoon, facing the opal waters of the Gulf of Mexico. Village boatmen will ferry you to and from the beach, and also offer flamingo tours. From the village there are fabulous sunsets (see p55 and p60).

Aké's mysterious columns

4 Aké

MAP C2 ▪ Open 8am–5pm daily ▪ Adm ▪ www.inah.gob.mx

This ruined city west of Izamal is a mystery, as its drum-shaped columns and ramp-like stairways are quite other Mayan buildings. The local church was built on an ancient Mayan pyramid (see p45). Alongside the ruins is an atmospheric 19th-century henequén hacienda, San Lorenzo de Aké, filled with vintage machinery.

Visitor exploring the magnificent Mayan site of Ek-Balam

⑤ Ek-Balam
MAP F2 ■ Open 8am–5pm daily
■ Adm ■ www.inah.gob.mx

In 1998, excavations revealed some of the finest examples of Mayan sculpture here, on the giant temple-mound known as the Acropolis. Most spectacular is El Trono (The Throne), a temple entrance believed to be the tomb of Ukit-Kan-Lek-Tok, who ruled around AD 800. Nearby is an intricate mass of finely carved figures. The rest of the Acropolis is a multilevel palace *(see p44)*.

⑥ Río Lagartos
MAP F1

This quiet village on the remote north coast is at the head of over 12 miles (20 km) of mangrove lagoon and mud flats, with the Yucatán's largest colonies of flamingos and a dazzling variety of other birds. Local boatmen offer good-value tours *(see p55 and p61)*.

Young eagle, Río Lagartos

⑦ Chichén Itzá

This is the most famous and awe-inspiring of all the great ancient Mayan cities, and the one with the most spine-tingling images of war and sacrifice. The great pyramid of El Castillo, the giant Ball Court, the Sacred Cenote, and the Temple of the Warriors are all must-sees *(see pp28–31)*.

⑧ Valladolid
MAP E3

The Spanish capital of the eastern Yucatán, founded in 1545, has at its heart one of the most charming of the region's colonial plazas, overlooked by the tall white cathedral. Valladolid is famed for embroidery, and the square is a good place to buy traditional white, flower-patterned *huípil* blouses and tablecloths. Around town are many more fine old Spanish churches and houses, including the beautifully renovated 17th-century townhouse, Casa de los Venados, housing a collection of contemporary Mexican folk art. Four blocks from the plaza you can look down into the dramatic pit of Cenote Zací, once Valladolid's main water source. Close by is the massive, fortress-like San Bernardino de Siena. Begun in 1552, it is the oldest permanent church in the Yucatán, with a beautifully shady gallery of graceful arches along the façade and a cloister of giant, squat stone columns set around a garden. Inside are some rare 18th-century Baroque altars and altarpieces *(see p48)*.

9 Telchac and Uaymitún
MAP C/D2

Far west of San Felipe, a road runs along the coast through quiet fishing villages. Seaward, there are endless, often empty, beaches; on the landward side is a lagoon full of birds. Telchac is a fishing harbor with fine beaches and a few cheap hotels and low-key restaurants. At Uaymitún there is a free observation tower for bird-watching in the lagoon *(see p55)*.

10 Izamal
MAP D2

The most unaltered Spanish colonial city in the Yucatán, known as *ciudad dorada* or "Golden City" for the color of its buildings, is centered on the huge San Antonio monastery, begun in 1549 and the shrine of Our Lady of Izamal, the region's patron. A short walk away are the remains of three pyramids, traces of a much older Mayan city *(see p46 and p48)*.

Golden-colored building, Izamal

THE SALT OF CHICHÉN

Salt was one of the greatest sources of wealth in ancient America. In the lagoons near Río Lagartos there are huge salt flats, still exploited today. Around AD 800, Chichén Itzá won control of them and built its own port at El Cerritos, east of Río Lagartos, to trade in salt. The wealth this gave Chichén was a major reason why it could dominate the Yucatán.

A TWO-DAY TOUR

▶ DAY ONE

Stay the night in **Valladolid**, or the little town of **Piste** (close to **Chichén Itza**), or better still one of the hotels just outside the sites such as **Hacienda Chichén** *(see p126)*. Get to the site as soon as possible to beat the crowds. You'll need at least three hours for exploring the site, before lunch at the charming **Las Mestizas** in Pisté *(see p107)*.

In the afternoon, make a choice: if you're interested in the ancient Maya, go up to **Ek-Balam**, or head into **Valladolid** for a wander around its plaza, San Bernardino monastery, and the dramatic town cenote. Before it's too late in the day, go north to Río Lagartos (65 miles/105 km) to reserve a flamingo tour for the next morning. Stay at the **Hotel San Felipe** in San Felipe *(see p131)*.

DAY TWO

The flamingos are best seen early, so you'll be off around 7am. A two- or four-hour tour takes you into an exuberant, rare natural world, through broad lagoons and narrow creeks. Afterward, for lunch, have a *ceviche* at Isla Contoy on the waterfront, or head to **Tizimín** *(see p104)* for steaks at the **Tres Reyes** *(see p107)* on its colonial square. From Tizimín, turn westward through miles and miles of cattle ranches to reach **Izamal**. Here you can look out on the town from the monastery's arcaded courtyard. The town's golden colors are especially lovely in the warm, early evening light.

The Best of the Rest

1 Ik Kil Cenote
MAP E3 ■ Highway 180,
2 miles (3 km) E of Chichén Itzá
■ Open 8am–5pm daily ■ Adm

A huge, circular pit filled with a beautiful underground pool – now the center of a private nature park. You can swim in the cenote pool and dine in the restaurant up above it.

2 Yaxcabá
MAP D3

This ultra sleepy little town in the woods surprises with its imposing 18th-century church, which features a unique three-tower façade and a beautifully carved wooden altarpiece.

3 Calotmul
MAP F2

Between Valladolid and Tizimín, this is another country town that has a fine church (1749) with a magnificently ornate Baroque altarpiece.

4 Tizimín
MAP F2

The hub of Yucatán's "cattle country" is a non-touristy market town. At its center are two spacious squares, divided by the massive walls of two Spanish monasteries (see p46).

5 Tihosuco
MAP E4 ■ Museum: Open
10am–6pm Tue–Sun ■ Adm

This remote village 30 miles (48 km) south of Valladolid was where the great Mayan revolt of the Caste War began (see p43); it still bears the battle scars. A small museum tells visitors the whole story.

6 El Cuyo
MAP F1

At the end of a lonely road through savanna, forest, and sand flats, this tiny fishing village is a place to enjoy miles of Gulf coast beaches (see p61).

7 Bocas de Dzilam
MAP D1

This vast area of mangroves west of San Felipe is remote and wild. There are no regular tours, but boatmen in San Felipe or Dzilam may offer a trip.

8 El Bajo and Santa Clara
MAP D1

Alongside the north coast road is a long, narrow sand-spit island, El Bajo, with deserted, coconut-palm shaded beaches. In the tiny village of Santa Clara you can find boatmen offering trips to the island.

9 Xcambó
MAP C2 ■ www.mayayucatan.com.mx ■ Open 8am–5pm daily ■ Adm

The atmospheric ruins of a coastal Mayan town, probably an outlying Dzibilchaltún settlement, with great views from the top of its pyramid.

10 Cenote Yokdzonot
MAP E3 ■ Yokdzonot village,
9 miles (14 km) west of Pisté ■ Open
9am–6pm daily ■ Adm

The little-visited village of Yokdzonot, a short drive from Pisté and Chichén Itzá, is home to a delightful, creeper-clad cenote, perfect for an afternoon dip. Life jackets and snorkeling gear are available.

Fortified church, Tihosuco

Shops, Markets, and Tours

1 **Main Plaza, Valladolid**
MAP E3

Mayan women from the surrounding villages display their beautifully bright *huípiles* (traditional blouses) and other embroidery on the railings of the Parque Principal.

2 **MexiGo Tours, Valladolid**
MAP E3 ■ (985) 856 0777
■ Calle 43, by Calle 40 and Calle 42
■ www.mexigotours.com

Owned and managed by locals, this outfitter offers guided tours for archaeological and historical sites in and around Valladolid. Bike rental is also available.

3 **Handicrafts Market, Chichén Itzá**
MAP E3

Around the Chichén Itzá visitor center there is something approaching a mall of handicrafts stalls, some of which are run by Maya selling their own embroidery, woven hammocks, and wood carvings.

4 **Flamingo Tours, Río Lagartos**
MAP F1 ■ (986) 862 0542

The best local boatmen's cooperative has a kiosk on the waterfront, just left of where the Tizimín road runs out. They work alongside the nature reserve and have good boats and experienced guides *(see p55)*.

5 **San Felipe Tours**
MAP E1 ■ (986) 100 8390

The boatmen's cooperative here is a bit less organized but also has a waterfront hut, in San Felipe village. Rates are similar to those in Río Lagartos, but boatmen here will be more ready to take you to the Bocas de Dzilam *(see p104)* and Río Lagartos lagoon *(see p55)*.

Handicrafts at Valladolid Market

6 **Valladolid Crafts Market and Bazaar**
MAP E3 ■ Mercado de Artesanías Calle 39, corner of Calle 44

Valladolid's semi-official handicrafts market has some fine embroidery, as well as more mass-produced goods. The nearby bazaar is a quirky set of shops around a food court *(see p107)*.

7 **Market, Tizimín**
MAP F2 ■ Open 8am–5pm daily

Not a place for souvenirs but a real, bustling country town market, with great fruit and produce and household goods.

8 **Yalat, Valladolid**
MAP E3 ■ Cnr of Calle 39 and Calle 40

Set on Valladolid's central plaza, Yalat offers jewelry, embroidered clothes, Mexican chocolate, and sisal-fiber bath scrubs.

Chichén Itzá

9 **Hecho a Mano, Izamal**
MAP D2 ■ Calle 31, No. 308, by the Town Hall

A pretty little shop with a more carefully selected display of handmade folk art than in the markets, as well as striking photographs of Yucatecan scenes.

10 **Market, Izamal**
MAP D2 ■ Calle 31/Calle 32

Izamal's market, just below the monastery, has a mix of souvenirs, handicrafts, and busy little cafés.

See map on pp100–101 ←

Drinking and Entertainment Spots

① La Chispa, Valladolid
MAP E3 ▪ Calle 41, between Calle 42 and Calle 44 ▪ $

A surprisingly stylish, youth-oriented bar-restaurant with smartly designed metallic fittings around the patio of an old colonial house.

② La Flor de Michoacán, Valladolid
MAP E3 ▪ Calle 41, between Calle 42 and Calle 44 ▪ $

Near the Chispa, this simple café, bakery, and ice-cream stand is a backpackers' favorite, and offers fresh juices and bargain snacks.

③ Sunday Concerts, Valladolid
MAP E3 ▪ Parque Principal ▪ From 7:30pm Sun

Like many Yucatán towns, Valladolid puts on entertainment for free – the town band gives a concert every Sunday night in the square, with a wide-ranging musical menu.

Hotel Maria de la Luz

④ Hotel María de la Luz, Valladolid
MAP E3 ▪ Calle 42 ▪ $$

This hotel has a big, well-shaded terrace on the Parque Principal, with very comfortable seats – ideal for lazy lounging while keeping an eye on all the movement in the square.

⑤ Squimz Bistro Café, Valladolid
MAP E3 ▪ Calle 39, No. 219, between Calle 44 and Calle 46 ▪ $

Located in an old colonial house, this bistro serves an interesting mix of Yucatecan and international cuisine. Their trademark dessert, Squimz's Flan Napolitano, is a must-have.

⑥ Pueblo Maya, Pisté
MAP E3 ▪ Calle 15, No. 48B, Manzana No. 13 ▪ $

Enjoy real Mexican food at Pueblo Maya, which is also a craft market. It has a lovely pool, and hammocks on which to lounge after your meal.

⑦ Miramar, El Cuyo
MAP F1 ▪ Calle 40, No. 3A ▪ Open 7am–8pm daily ▪ $

Part of Hotel Aida Luz in the tranquil fishing village of El Cuyo, Miramar serves Yucatecan dishes made with locally caught fish.

⑧ Ria Maya, Río Lagartos
MAP F1 ▪ (986) 862 0045 ▪ Calle 19, by Calle 13 and Calle 14 ▪ $$

Popular for its seafood, the menu at this family-friendly restaurant is complemented not only by its settings but also fine sunset views.

⑨ Market Bars, Izamal
MAP D2 ▪ Calle 31, by Calle 32 ▪ $

Several cafés and *loncherías* here share an outside terrace, a fine vantage point on the monastery and town life. Some serve beer; some only soft drinks with their snacks.

⑩ Hacienda Chichén
MAP E3 ▪ Hotel Zone, Chichén Itzá ▪ $$$

This historic ranch-hotel, on the fringes of the Chichén Itzá site, has a delightful terrace restaurant-bar that is perfect for a cooling cocktail after a day spent exploring the site.

Places to Eat

PRICE CATEGORIES
For a three-course meal for one with a beer of soda (or equivalent meal), taxes and extra charges.

$ under $15 $$ $15–$35 $$$ over $35

1 Restaurante El Toro, Izamal

MAP D2 ▪ Plazuela 2 de Abril ▪ (998) 954 1169 ▪ No credit cards ▪ $

Set on a square near the monastery is this friendly little restaurant, with tasty Yucatecan dishes and tacos.

2 Cocinas Económicas, Valladolid
MAP E3 ▪ Calle 39, on Parque Principal ▪ No credit cards ▪ $

Around the bazaar on the square (see p105) there's a line of self-service food counters. Noisy, with lots of atmosphere, this is a great place for a good breakfast, and to try out local snacks.

3 Casa Italia, Valladolid
MAP E3 ▪ Calle 35, No. 202 ▪ $

Overlooking a quaint plaza a short walk from the city centre, this family-run restaurant serves the best Italian food in Valladolid, drawing a loyal crowd of locals and visitors. The thin-crust pizzas and pasta dishes are authentic and good value.

4 Chaya's Natural Café, Ek-Balam
MAP F2 ▪ Off the northeast corner of the town plaza ▪ $$

The restaurant at Genesis Retreat (see p129) is open to non-guests only in the afternoon, but the crêpes and chocolate-chili cookies make it well worth a visit.

5 Las Mestizas, Pisté

MAP E3 ▪ (985) 851 0069 ▪ No credit cards ▪ $$

The prettiest of the restaurants along the main road in Pisté, with charming service. It dishes up a delicious sopa de lima (see p69).

6 Hostería del Marqués, Valladolid
MAP E3 ▪ Calle 39, on Parque Principal ▪ (985) 856 3042 ▪ $$

Valladolid's best hotel also has its most eminent restaurant, with tables around a plant-filled patio. Its versions of local specialties like *lomitos de Valladolid* are definitive.

Patio dining at Hostería del Marqués

7 Tres Reyes, Tizimín

MAP F2 ▪ Calle 52, corner of Calle 53 ▪ (986) 863 2106 ▪ No credit cards ▪ $$

The specialty of the Yucatán cattle capital's best restaurant is steak, often cooked in thin strips (*arracheras*).

8 Yerba Buena del Sisal, Valladolid
MAP E3 ▪ Calle 54A No. 217 ▪ (985) 856 1406 ▪ $

This charming restaurant is decorated with *papel picado* banners and is a great option for vegetarians.

9 Restaurante Vaselina, San Felipe
MAP E1 ▪ (986) 862 2083 ▪ $$

A big, unfussy, place on the seafront where you can try wonderfully fresh, fat shrimp, octopus, and conch.

10 Kinich, Izamal

MAP D2 ▪ Calle 27, No. 299, between Calle 28 and Calle 30 ▪ (988) 954 0489 ▪ Closed D ▪ $$

Set in a lush garden, this place has a high reputation for classic Yucatecan food, such as *poc-chuc* (see p68).

See map on pp100–101

🔟 The West

Arch of Labná

Nowhere is the flavor of the Yucatán more intense than in the west of the region, around its historic capital, Mérida. In these parts, there is an extraordinary density of Mayan relics and, although they may not match the awe-inspiring power of Chichén Itzá, sites such as Uxmal show the architecture of the Maya at its most elegant. Beyond the main sights are stretches of wilderness, hidden lagoons, and small towns dripping with bougainvillea and hibiscus.

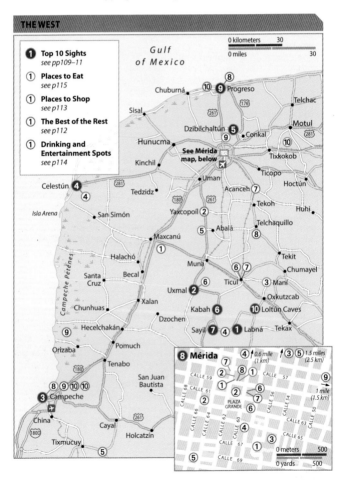

1 Labná
MAP C4 ■ Open 8am–5pm daily ■ Adm

The Arch of Labná, wonderfully drawn by Frederick Catherwood (see p110), exemplifies the sophistication of Puuc architecture. Nearby, the town's Palacio is only slightly smaller than Sayil's, and was divided into seven patios – the part to the left (west) was the home of the lords of Labná, while the patios to the right were for servants. The setting, in tranquil woods full of birds, is especially lovely.

2 Uxmal
With the elegant lines of the Nunnery Quadrangle and towering mass of the Pyramid of the Magician, Uxmal is not only one of the most beautiful of ancient Mayan cities but also one of the greatest sights in the Americas (see pp34–5).

3 Campeche
This Spanish colonial walled city retains a charming old-world feel. The 17th-century ramparts and bastions were built to defend it against pirates. The streets within are lined with delicately colored old houses featuring patios and iron-grilled windows. A museum, housed in an old Spanish fort, contains jade funeral masks and other fine relics from the excavated site at Calakmul (see pp38–9).

Colorful colonial Campeche

Flamingos at Celestún

4 Celestún
MAP A3 ■ Tours from Celestún Embarcadero: Open 8am–5pm daily ■ Adm

Just north of this fishing village is a silent, watery expanse of mangrove lagoon that is a breeding ground for flamingos, ibises, egrets, and blue herons. Boat tours are very popular (the lagoon can get rather crowded at times). Stay over in Celestún after the tours have gone back to Mérida to enjoy this tranquil village, with its white beach, laid-back restaurants and hotels, and fabulous sunsets.

STEPHENS AND CATHERWOOD

The existence of an ancient Mayan civilization was brought to the world's attention by the American traveler John Lloyd Stephens (1805–52) and English artist Frederick Catherwood (1799–1854). Traveling together from 1839 to 1842, they provided the first full descriptions and drawings of Chichén Itzá and Uxmal, and are credited with the discovery of Kabah and Sayil, among others.

Cenote Xlacah, Dzibilchaltún

5 Dzibilchaltún

MAP C2 ■ Cenote Xlacah: open 8am–5pm daily ■ Adm Mon–Fri

The Temple of the Seven Dolls, through which the sun strikes at dawn on spring and fall equinoxes to run straight along a white *sacbé* (rough cast road) to the central plaza, is the most celebrated feature of this Mayan city just north of Mérida. It was one of the longest-inhabited Mayan cities, occupied for over 2,000 years. There are additional temples at the site, as well as a grand Palacio and a Spanish missionary chapel. The huge, mysterious pool – Cenote Xlacah – which provided the ancient city with water, now offers an idyllic place in which to cool off.

6 Kabah

MAP C4 ■ Open 8am–5pm daily ■ Adm

This was the second most important of the Puuc cities (see p37) after Uxmal, and an imposing arch on its west side marks the start of the *sacbé* road (see p93) that linked it to its larger ally. Its Codz Poop, or "Palace of Masks," is the most extravagant example of Mayan carving: the extraordinary facade is covered with 250 faces of the long-nosed rain-god Chac. The Palacio and Temple of the Columns are two more classics of refined Puuc architecture.

7 Sayil

MAP C4 ■ Open 8am–5pm daily ■ Adm

Of all the Puuc cities, Sayil is the one that gives the strongest sense of the huge wealth of its ancient inhabitants. Its hub is the magnificent Palacio, an opulent complex that sweeps up through three levels and more than 90 chambers, with an architectural refinement that recalls the buildings of ancient Greece. It housed over 350 people, from lords to servants, and had its own exclusive water supply.

8 Mérida

This is perhaps the most seductive of all the colonial cities in Mexico, with elegant architecture,

Sunday fiesta in Mérida

shady patios, great markets, and a distinct friendliness. With the soft music of *boleros* and the *jarana* heard in free concerts in 16th-century squares, and fiestas enjoyed by all ages every Sunday, the town's appeal is plentiful and varied *(see pp32–3)*.

Progreso's dramatic pier

⑨ Progreso

Mérida's port and favorite beach town is a place to get close to ordinary Yucatecan life. The harbor is set at the end of a 4-mile (6-km) pier, and so the shallow waters around the beach remain blissfully tranquil. It's calm until the weekend, that is, when Meridanos spill out onto the sand and into the warm blue waters. There are excellent fish restaurants along the seafront, too, with large, convivial outside terraces on which to socialize.

⑩ Loltún Caves

MAP C4 ■ Tours 8–11am and 2–4pm Mon–Sat, 8–11am Sun ■ Adm

This vast cave complex is both a stunning natural phenomenon and an ancient Mayan site. It has been occupied by humans longer than anywhere else in the Yucatán, from remote prehistory right up until the 19th century. The ancient Maya lived here, mined the caves, and used them for rituals. Guided tours take you through 1.5 miles (2 km) of caves, but the network extends much further. The rock formations are awe-inspiring, and a special feature of Loltún is its strange changes of temperature, from fierce heat to chilly breezes *(see p59)*.

A DAY IN THE PUUC HILLS

▶ **MORNING**

Leave **Mérida** early in a rental car and drive directly to **Uxmal** *(see pp34–5)*. Beyond the suburb of Umán, where you turn onto Highway 261, traffic thins out, and you'll have an easy drive through woods and a few tranquil villages.

Beyond Muna the road enters the Puuc Hills before descending to Uxmal. Spend at least two hours exploring this site, keeping an eye out for the many iguanas as well as admiring the architecture.

Recoup your energies by heading back up the road to the nearby **Hacienda Uxmal** *(see p115)* for *sopa de lima* on the terrace.

AFTERNOON

Head straight for **Kabah** to marvel at the monsters of the Codz Poop.

Further south, the "Puuc Route" turns off the main Highway 261 onto a lovely woodland road, with only a few other tourists, tricycle carts, and the birds for company. Along the way are stop-offs at the Puuc sites of **Sayil**, **Xlapak** *(see p45)*, and **Labná** *(see p109)*. At the end of the road, descend into the netherworld of the **Loltún Caves**, refreshing yourself afterwards in the café.

Go down to Oxkutzcab, and turn left for **Ticul** *(see p112)*, where you can take a leisurely stroll around its historic Plaza Mayor. Drive back to Mérida, stopping en route at **Yaxcopoil** *(see p112)* for a quick tour of the hacienda.

See map on p108 ←

The Best of the Rest

1 Oxkintok
MAP B3 ■ www.inah.gob.mx
■ Open 8am–5pm daily ■ Adm

This ancient Mayan city has a Satunsat, or "Labyrinth" pyramid, containing a strange, dark maze, possibly built as an entrance to the Underworld that only the Lord of Oxkintok could use.

2 Yaxcopoíl Hacienda
MAP C3 ■ www.yaxcopoil.com
■ Open 8am–6pm Mon–Sat, 9am–1pm Sun ■ Adm

Of all the restored haciendas in the Yucatán, this one, with its crumbling, ornate main house and factory buildings, gives the best feel of life here when henequén or "green gold" (see p43) dominated the state.

3 Cenotes
The cenotes and underwater rivers in the western Yucatán are far less well explored than those around Tulum (see pp22–3). Snorkeling and diving trips are run from Mérida.

4 Xlapak
MAP C4 ■ www.inah.gob.mx
■ Open 8am–5pm daily ■ Adm

The smallest Puuc site is as attractive for the undisturbed woodland walk as for its archaeological site. The little Palacio has intricate Puuc carving (see p37).

5 Edzná
MAP B5 ■ www.inah.gob.mx
■ Open 8am–5pm daily ■ Adm

This is a Mayan city as spectacular as Chichén Itzá. The "Building of the Five Stories" is one of the largest Mayan palaces (see p39).

Ochre-colored church in Ticul

6 Ticul
MAP C4

One of the most charming Yucatán country towns (see also p47), Ticul is also a historic center for ceramics.

7 Acanceh
MAP C3

On one side of the square of this remarkable little town is an 18th-century church, while on another is a very ancient Mayan pyramid, perhaps begun around 300 BC (see p47).

8 Mayapán
MAP C3 ■ www.inah.gob.mx
■ Open 8am–5pm daily ■ Adm

The last big Mayan city, and one that dominated the Yucatán for 200 years after 1200. Its buildings often "mimic" Chichén Itzá and have beautifully preserved frescoes.

9 The Campeche Petenés
MAP A4

This mangrove and forest wilderness is home to a wide range of wildlife such as pumas and turtles. Trips can be arranged from Campeche or the village of Isla Arena (see p55).

10 Chelem and Yucalpetén
MAP C2

Just west of Progreso, on the other side of a gap in the coastal sand bar, these easy-going villages have long, almost empty beaches. They're popular for windsurfing.

The site of Edzná

Places to Shop

1 Bazar de Artesanías Craft Market, Mérida

MAP C2 ■ Calle 67, by corner of Calle 56

This semi-official handicrafts market is packed with stalls selling every kind of Yucatecan and Mexican craft work, some of it excellent, and some rather tatty.

2 Casa de Artesanías, Mérida

MAP C2 ■ Calle 63, No. 503, between Calle 64 and Calle 66

The Yucatán state handicrafts store has high-quality local work, with many beautiful, usable things especially in textiles, basketware, and wood.

3 Mérida Market

MAP C2 ■ Calle 65, between Calle 54 and Calle 58

One of the world's greatest markets, this is a labyrinth of alleys and stalls selling everything imaginable – fish, fruit, a huge range of chilies, *huipil* blouses, sandals, and hats.

4 Hamacas La Poblana, Mérida

MAP C2 ■ Calle 65, No. 492, Centro

Street stalls sell cheap but poor-quality hammocks – head here for the real thing in every color, size, and style, sold by weight.

5 El Charro Mexicano, Mérida

MAP C2 ■ 59 515, Zona Paseo Montejo, La Quinta

A little shop selling *botas* (boots) and *sombreros* (hats) opposite the market, with a friendly owner who will show you piles of handmade panamas in all sorts of styles and sizes.

6 Mexicanísimo, Mérida

MAP C2 ■ Parque Hidalgo Calle 60, between Calle 59 and Calle 61

This is an innovative store that sells lightweight clothes for men and women in original, modern designs, using Mexican cottons and other traditional materials.

7 Arte Maya, Ticul

MAP C4 ■ Calle 23, No. 301

Ticul produces huge quantities of ceramics. This family-run store stands out for the owners' skills and careful use of traditional and even ancient Mayan techniques.

8 Guayaberas Jack, Mérida

MAP C2 ■ Calle 59, No. 507, between Calle 60 and Calle 62

The *guayabera* shirt-jacket is the smartest thing for gentlemen to wear in tropical Mérida. This long-established shop sells only *guayaberas*, and can make them to measure.

9 Maya Chuy Bordado, Mérida

MAP C2 ■ Calle 18, No. 80

This charming shop, tucked away from the crowded shopping streets of Mérida, is the outlet of a women's embroidery cooperative. Blouses, rugs, and other items are beautifully and individually made.

Mérida market pottery

10 Casa de Artesanías Tukulná, Campeche

MAP A5 ■ Calle 10, No. 333, between Calle 59 and Calle 61

Campeche's state handicrafts store has a great choice of ceramics, embroidery, basketwork, and many other top-quality items that are beautifully displayed.

See map on p108

Drinking and Entertainment Spots

① Pancho's, Mérida
MAP C2 ▪ Calle 59, No. 509, between Calle 60 and Calle 62 ▪ $

The liveliest, most enjoyable dance club and bar-restaurant in central Mérida has Mexican bandit decor, welcoming staff, and a tiny, buzzing open-air dance floor (see p67).

② Dulcería y Sorbetería El Colón, Mérida
MAP C2 ▪ Calle 59, on the plaza ▪ $

Choose from a huge array of fruit-flavored sorbets and ice creams at this plaza-front parlor. A popular order is a *champola*, scoops of fruit ice served in a tall glass with milk.

③ El Cielo Lounge Bar, Mérida
MAP C2 ▪ Prolongación Paseo de Montejo, at Calle 25 ▪ $

A lounge bar with minimalist decor, El Cielo has a lovely terrace and an extensive drinks menu.

④ Café Crème, Mérida
MAP C2 ▪ Calle 41, corner of Calle 60 Centro ▪ $$

Located in downtown Mérida, two blocks from Paseo Montejo, Café Crème serves a variety of tasty French snacks and refreshing natural fruit juices.

⑤ Ku'uk, Mérida
MAP C2 ▪ Av Rómulo Rozo No. 488, by Calle 27 and Calle 27A ▪ (999) 944 3377 ▪ $$$

Indulge in the superlative tasting menu at this upscale restaurant or simply relax with a cocktail at its sophisticated bar. There is also a fine collection of wine and beer, with many sourced from around Mexico.

⑥ Jugos California, Mérida
MAP C2 ▪ Calle 58, No. 505 Centro ▪ $

Juice stands are a wonderful local institution, and Jugos California wins the prize as the best in town. You'll find a mouthwatering array of watermelons, pineapples, papayas, and more all waiting to be juiced.

Courtyard bar of Piedra de Agua

⑦ Piedra de Agua, Mérida
MAP C2 ▪ Calle 62, No. 498 ▪ $$

In a boutique hotel of the same name, close to the Santa Lucia church, this welcoming courtyard bar is a classy spot for an evening cocktail, glass of wine, or ice-cold beer.

⑧ Flamingos, Progreso
MAP C2 ▪ Malecón, corner of Calle 22 ▪ $$

One of Progreso's most enjoyable big terrace bar-restaurants, with tasty *ceviches* (see p69) to go with the beer.

⑨ Casa Vieja de los Arcos, Campeche
MAP A5 ▪ Calle 10, No. 319, Altos on the plaza ▪ $$

Watch the sun set from the balcony of this Cuban restaurant-bar on Campeche's central square. Enjoy their signature minty Mojitos made with Cuban rum.

⑩ La Parroquia, Campeche
MAP A5 ▪ Calle 55, No. 8 ▪ $$

Traditional local delicacies are served for breakfast, lunch, and dinner at this popular restaurant with a well-deserved reputation.

Places to Eat

① Amaro, Mérida
MAP C2 ∎ Calle 59, No. 507,
between Calle 60 and Calle 62
∎ (999) 928 2451 ∎ $$

One of old Mérida's loveliest patios
houses this relaxing restaurant,
which has a half-vegetarian menu,
including several dishes made with
the Yucatecan vegetable *chaya*.

② El Marlin Azul, Mérida
MAP C2 ∎ Calle 62, No. 488,
between Calle 57 and Calle 59 ∎ (999)
928 1606 ∎ $$

Ceviche is the dish to order at this
seafood restaurant but also try the
shrimp fajitas. Go for lunch, as it
closes at 4pm *(see p70)*.

③ El Príncipe Tutul-Xiu, Maní
MAP C4 ∎ Calle 26 No. 208, between
Calle 25 and Calle 27 ∎ (999) 929
7721 ∎ $$

Set under a giant *palapa* roof, this
restaurant is busiest on Sundays,
when families drive from Mérida to
eat *poc-chuc*, *panuchos*, and other
Yucatecan staples *(see pp68–9)*.

④ La Palapa, Celestún
MAP A3 ∎ Calle 12, by corner
of Calle 11 ∎ (988) 916 2063 ∎ $$

Automatic first choice in Celestún, a
comfortable beach terrace beneath
a *palapa* roof, serving up succulent,
coriander-rich platters of octopus,
fish, and shrimp.

⑤ Hacienda Ochil
MAP C3 ∎ Off Highway 261,
signposted about 25 miles (40 km)
from Mérida ∎ (999) 924 7465 ∎ $$

This restaurant in a restored hacienda
offers traditional Yucatecan dishes
on a delightful terrace.

⑥ Hacienda Uxmal, Uxmal
MAP C4 ∎ Antigua Carretera
Mérida–Campeche km 78 ∎ $$$

Located opposite the site of Uxmal,
this restaurant has a tropical garden
and ethnic artworks, and serves fine
local and international cuisine.

⑦ La Chaya Maya, Mérida
MAP C2 ∎ Corner of Calle 62
and Calle 57, between 60 and 62 ∎ $$

An oasis of high-quality, reasonably
priced Yucatecan food, amid its more
costly neighbors. Dishes range from
salbutes to *cochinita pibil (see p71)*.

⑧ La Pigua, Campeche
MAP A5 ∎ Alemán No. 179A
∎ $$

Taking advantage of Campeche's
prime position on the Gulf of Mexico,
La Pigua serves super-fresh fish
and seafood in understated but
sophisticated surroundings.

Casa de Piedra, Xcanatún

⑨ Casa de Piedra, Xcanatún
MAP C2 ∎ Xcanatún, 7 miles (12 km)
N of Mérida ∎ (999) 941 0213 ∎ $$$

A comfortable hacienda restaurant in
a garden, Casa de Piedra combines
local and Caribbean cooking with a
few French touches *(see p71)*.

⑩ Hacienda San José Cholul
MAP C2 ∎ Hwy Tixkokob–Tekanto,
km 30 ∎ (999) 924 1333 ∎ $$$

Set in a lovely colonial hacienda, the
biggest draw is the secluded garden.
The service is also excellent.

See map on p108

Streetsmart

Colorful colonial buildings
in Campeche's old walled city

Getting To and Around Cancún and the Yucatán

Arriving by Air

There are frequent direct daily flights from cities across Canada and the U.S. to Cancún and the Yucatán. From the U.K. or mainland Europe, you generally have to travel via the U.S. or Mexico City, although there are a few scheduled flights, plus several charter services during the high seasons. There are frequent flights between Mexico City and regional airports. Airlines that fly to the area include major carriers such as **American Airlines** and **United Airlines**, as well as **Aeroméxico**, **Interjet**, **Magnicharters**, **Viva Aerobus**, **Air Europa**, and **Volaris**.

Cancún Airport, 9 miles (15 km) south of the city, near the southernmost point of Cancún Island, is the main international airport in the Yucatán. *Colectivo* minibuses are the easiest means of public transport from the airport to the city. They take an hour, traveling along the Hotel Zone and into Ciudad (Downtown) Cancún, dropping each passenger at their hotel. Airport taxis can be hard to find. However, when you are departing for the airport, any Cancún city cab can take you there.

There are also public transport services from Cancún airport to various other destinations. The Riviera Maya bus leaves for Puerto Morelos and Playa del Carmen almost hourly between 10:30am and 7pm. There are also hourly *colectivos* from outside the domestic arrivals hall, 6am–6pm. If you're going anywhere else on the coast, take the bus to Playa del Carmen and continue from there.

Both Cozumel and Mérida airports also have international connections. **Cozumel Airport** is just north of San Miguel town; **Mérida Airport** is about 3 miles (4 km) southwest of the city centre; taxis and *colectivos* are available from both airports.

Arriving by Road

When driving from the U.S. you will need a Tourist Card if you are planning to travel beyond the 12-mile (20-km) border zone and to stay for more than 72 hours. You should also obtain Mexican insurance and a Temporary Import Permit for your vehicle, which is valid for six months. Allow five days or so to drive from the Texas border to the Yucatán. However, it's worth noting that most U.S. car-rental companies will not allow their cars to be driven in to Mexico. Bear in mind that the US–Mexico border, especially around Ciudad Juárez and Tijuana, is a hotspot in Mexico's drugs war, so it is essential to exercise extra caution.

Getting Around by Bus

Buses are the main form of transport for longer trips in the Yucatán, unless you rent a car or fly. First-class buses are air-conditioned and run between main cities and towns with only a few stops en route. Second-class buses are cheaper, a bit less comfortable, and stop more often. Every city and most towns have a local bus service. Destinations are usually displayed on the windscreen, but **Cancún buses** will show route numbers (routes R-1 and R-2 run up and down the Hotel Zone and to Ciudad Cancún). *Colectivos*, also known as *combis*, are minibuses that serve the smaller and outlying districts and generally depart when full.

Getting Around by Ferry

Passenger ferries run to Isla Mujeres from Puerto Juárez, which is just north of Cancún, at intervals of every half hour or so daily. Fast boats will get you there in around 20 minutes. There are also several daily car ferries from Punta Sam, north of Puerto Juárez. Shuttle boats run from points along Cancún beach, too.

Passenger ferries operated by **Ultramar** and **Mexico Waterjets** run roughly every two hours between Playa del Carmen and Cozumel. The journey takes about 45 minutes. A Cozumel shuttle boat runs from Playa Tortugas or Muelle Fiscal in Cancún.

The car ferry, which runs from Puerto Morelos to

Cozumel, is infrequent and expensive.

Getting Around by Taxi

Taxis in Cancún and the Yucatán don't tend to have meters, but instead charge official set rates for each locality. In Cancún, the official rates are significantly higher for trips to and from anywhere in the Hotel Zone than in Ciudad Cancún.

Note that cab drivers in some places, particularly Cancún, Playa del Carmen, and Tulum, have a bad reputation for charging foreigners exaggerated rates. The complicated official pricing system in Cancún, where there are different prices for the Hotel Zone and Ciudad Cancún, also makes scams easier.

Wherever you are going, always agree upon a price before getting into the cab, and firmly refuse any outrageous demands.

Getting Around by Car

A car makes getting to the Mayan ruins and the more isolated beaches in the region much easier. There are plenty of rental offices along the Riviera Maya, including global agencies **Avis** and **Alamo**, but if you are traveling around the Yucatán, it is best to rent in Mérida, whose smaller agencies tend to charge lower rates. To rent a car you must be over 21 and have your driving license, passport, and a credit card. Jeeps are popular, as some of the more remote roads are unpaved.

Prices are usually higher than in the U.S. but lower than in Europe for both unleaded (*magna* or high-grade premium) and diesel. Occasionally, gas station attendants start the pump with *pesos* already on the gauge. To avoid this, get out of the car and check the pump first. The attendant should then demonstrate that it is set at zero. In rural areas, gas stations are few and far between, so fill up whenever you can.

There are two fast toll highways in the Yucatán – the 180-Cuota part of the route between Cancún and Mérida, and another stretch from Campeche to Champotón. Tolls are relatively high, so many drivers prefer the parallel old road (180–Libre).

The main peculiarity of driving in Mexico is the *tope*, or speed bump, designed to make the streets safer for pedestrians. Although they are usually signposted, they are very steep and can catch drivers unawares, causing damage to vehicles going at any speed above a crawl.

Night also falls very quickly in the tropics, and there is no lighting at all in country areas. *Topes*, potholes, and people on bicycles can rapidly become hazardous.

Getting Around on Foot

Old Yucatán towns like Mérida, Campeche, and Valladolid are fairly compact, and strolling around is the best way to get to know them. Mechanized transport is only really essential in Cancún.

Getting Around by Other Means

Many resorts have golf carts and scooters for hire. Cancún has a dedicated cycle track all along the Hotel Zone, and hotels often have guest bikes.

DIRECTORY

ARRIVING BY AIR

Aeroméxico
w aeromexico.com

Air Europa
w aireuropa.com

American Airlines
w aa.com

Cancún Airport
w cancun-airport.com

Cozumel Airport
w cozumelairport.org

Interjet
w interjet.com.mx

Magnicharters
w magnicharters.com.mx

Mérida Airport
w asur.com.mx/en/airports/merida

United Airlines
w united.com

Viva Aerobus
w vivaaerobus.com

Volaris
w volaris.com/en

GETTING AROUND BY BUS

Cancún buses
w cancun.travel/en

GETTING AROUND BY FERRY

Mexico Waterjets
w mexicowaterjets.com

Ultramar
w granpuerto.com.mx

GETTING AROUND BY CAR

Alamo
w alamo.com.mx

Avis
w avis.mx

Practical Information

Passports and Visas

Citizens of Canada, the U.S., the U.K., Ireland, EU states, Australia, and New Zealand do not require visas for stays of up to six months in Mexico.

All visitors must fill in a tourist card, which will be stamped with the length of your permitted stay, from 30 days to six months. Make sure you keep it with your passport, as it is collected at check-in when you leave. If you want to stay more than 30 days, ask the immigration officer or apply for an extension at the **Immigration Office** at Cancún Airport. Entry requirements do sometimes change, so check the latest situation before traveling to Mexico.

The U.K., U.S., Canada, and other countries have consular representation in the region. There are **U.S. consulates** in Cancún, Mérida, and Playa del Carmen. The **Canada consulate** and **U.K. consulate** are in Cancún.

Customs Regulations

All tourists must fill in a customs form on arrival. There are restrictions on the import of plants, perishable foods, and especially firearms, which will be confiscated without compensation.

Travel Safety Advice

Visitors can get up-to-date travel safety information from the **U.S. Department of State**, from the **Australian Department of Foreign Affairs and Trade**, and from the **U.K. Foreign and Commonwealth Office**.

Travel Insurance

Take out a comprehensive travel insurance policy covering cancellations, loss of baggage, theft, and all medical eventualities, including repatriation. If you plan to go scuba diving during your holiday you may need additional cover, so check your policy carefully before you leave home.

Health

There are no obligatory inoculations for travelers to Mexico, but it is advisable to be immunized against typhoid, tetanus, polio, and hepatitis A. If you are heading into forest or jungle areas elsewhere in Mexico or Central America, consult your doctor about malaria pills. Take a basic first-aid kit with you, including bite cream, antiseptic wipes, and remedies to deal with upset stomachs.

If you need medical care, and have full travel health insurance, visit a private clinic, such as **AmeriMed** in Cancún or the **Centro Médico de las Américas** in Mérida, both of which employ English-speaking staff.

In small towns and rural areas, basic public health centres (centros de salud) have emergency facilities. All Mexican villages and towns will have pharmacies, often open 24 hours a day, and these stock a huge range of medications.

The quality of tap water has improved greatly, particularly in Cancún. To be on the safe side, however, it's best to drink only bottled or purified water (agua purificada). Most restaurants and bars use it to make ice, although it never hurts to check beforehand.

Mangroves are breeding grounds for mosquitoes, which are most active in the early evening, when they spread into neighboring areas – especially around Sian Ka'an, on Isla Holbox, and around watery areas and cenotes behind the coast near Tankah, Puerto Morelos, and some other points on the Riviera. The best way to avoid bites is to stay away from those areas at dusk. Although mosquitos in the Yucatán are not malarial, covering up and using bug repellent is essential. The most effective products will contain DEET. You will have a better choice of repellents if you buy before you come to Mexico.

Personal Security

The Yucatán is generally fairly tranquil, but be wary of pickpocketing and petty crime. There is a certain amount of street hassle in Cancún, Mérida, and Playa del Carmen, while cheaper cabañas are sometimes subject to break-ins. Lone women should be careful in Playa del Carmen and in parts of Cancún and Tulum.

It is wise to avoid empty streets at night, lonely beaches around Playa, and obscure areas of Mayan sites.

In tourist areas there are often kiosks with eager staff buttonholing tourists and asking if they want "information." They are actually selling tours or timeshares, so stick to the official tourist offices (see p123).

September to November is when hurricanes are most likely to hit. Mexico has in place extensive anti-hurricane precautions, and many buildings in Cancún and the Riviera have orange signs that identify them as an official Refugio Anticiclón, to be used as public hurricane shelter when necessary. Most waters around the Yucatán are placid, but take special care on the eastern beaches of Isla Mujeres and Cozumel and on the surf beaches of Cancún Island, where the seas are rougher and there can be a fairly strong undertow. Check the warning flags before swimming (blue is safe; yellow means use caution; red means don't swim).

Along the Riviera are several high-standard emergency facilities for divers, all linked to qualified dive-masters.

Emergency Services

There are central phone numbers for **emergency** services in Cancún and Mérida, but in general it is better to call the local police directly, or the **Red Cross** in case of medical emergencies. In Cancún, private English-speaking clinics also have emergency ambulances. If you are staying in a hotel, your concierge will be able to make a call for you, either for a doctor to visit you at the hotel or for a taxi or an ambulance to take you to a hospital

In most towns, the police station is normally located near the main square or next to the town hall. Cancún and Mérida (and a few other towns) also have dedicated **Tourist Police** (Policía Turística) units that have some English-speaking officers on their staff.

DIRECTORY

PASSPORTS AND VISAS

Canadian Consular Agency, Cancún
Centro Empresarial Oficina E7, Blvd, Kukulcan km 12, Hotel Zone, 77599 Cancún
[C] (998) 883 3360
[W] mexico.gc.ca

Immigration Office
Cancún Airport
Open 24 hrs Mon–Fri
[C] (998) 848 7200

U.K. Consulate, Cancún
The Royal Sands Resort, Blvd Kukulcan km 13.5, Hotel Zone, 77500 Cancún
[C] (998) 881 0100
[W] ukinmexico.fco.gov.uk

U.S. Consulate, Cancún
Torre La Europea, Blvd Kukulcan km 13, Hotel Zone, 77500 Cancún
[C] (998) 883 0272
[W] mx.usembassy.gov

U.S. Consulate, Mérida
Calle 60, No. 338, at Calle 29 and 31, Col. Alcala Martin, 97050 Merida
[C] (999) 942 5700
[W] mx.usembassy.gov

U.S. Consulate, Playa Del Carmen
"The Palapa," Calle 1 Sur, between Av 15 and 20, Playa del Carmen
[C] (984) 873 0303
[W] mx.usembassy.gov

TRAVEL SAFETY ADVICE

Australian Department of Foreign Affairs and Trade
[W] dfat.gov.au/
[W] smartraveller.gov.au/

U.K. Foreign and Commonwealth Office
[W] gov.uk/foreign-travel-advice

U.S. Department of State
[W] travel.state.gov

HEALTH

AmeriMed, Cancún
Av Plaza las Américas Bonampak, Cancún
[C] (998) 881 3400
[W] amerimedcancun.com

Centro Médico de las Américas, Mérida
Calle 54, No. 365, nr Paseo Montejo, Mérida
[C] (999) 926 2111
[W] centromedicodelas americas.com.mx

EMERGENCY SERVICES

Emergency, Cancún
[C] 060

Emergency, Mérida
[C] 066

Red Cross, Cancún
[C] 065 or (998) 884 1616

Red Cross, Mérida
[C] (999) 924 9813 (Mérida)

Tourist Police, Cancún
[C] 066

Tourist Police, Mérida
[C] 066 or (999) 983 1184

Currency and Banking

Mexico's currency is the peso. The usual symbol for the peso is the same as the dollar sign; prices quoted in US dollars usually have the prefix US$ or suffix USD.

Many businesses on the Riviera also accept USD, and many tourists use only USD during their trip. Note, though, that USD prices usually work out higher than pesos.

Most banks have at least one ATM, although they can be hard to find in rural areas. All tourist areas have numerous small foreign-exchange offices (cambios).

MasterCard and VISA are widely accepted for larger purchases in hotels of mid-range level and above, in stores, and at diving schools; American Express is less popular. Credit cards are virtually essential for car rentals, but some restaurants and most smaller shops don't accept them.

Hotel and restaurant listings in this book are given in US dollars.

Telephone and Internet

To make a call anywhere in Mexico outside of your local area, first dial 01, then the three-digit area code, 998 for Cancún, 997 for Playa del Carmen, or 999 for Mérida (given with all numbers in this guide) followed by the number. Within the same area code, you need only dial the seven-digit number. For all calls to cell phones first dial 044. To call outside Mexico, dial 00 followed by the country code. To call Mexico from abroad, the code is 52.

White, long-distance (lada) payphones are common across the region. Most accept tarjetas de teléfonos, phone cards that are widely available. In every village, there is always a caseta, or phone office. Internet cafés are also common, and most hotels and many restaurants and bars have Wi-Fi.

Postal Services

Stamps (estampillas) can also be bought at any shop with an Expendio de Estampillas sign. The Mexican mail service is very erratic – for anything of importance, it is best to use the **Mexpost** courier service, available at main post offices.

TV, Radio, and the Press

Most hotels have cable or satellite TV with several English-language news, sports, and entertainment channels, the majority of them American. With a short-wave radio you can pick up **Voice of America**.

The **Mexico News Daily** has a useful website. The Spanish-language **Diario de Yucatán** daily newspaper has information on local fiestas and events. Free English-language magazines, including **Cancún Tips**, Cozumel's **Free Blue Guide**, **Yucatán Today** in Mérida, and Playa del Carmen's **The Playa Times**, can be found in tourist offices, hotels, and cafés. They also have maps of their areas.

Opening Hours

Most shops open around 8:30am and close at 9pm from Monday to Saturday, with the more traditional ones closing for lunch 1–3pm. Markets usually open very early, before 8am, and close by 2–3pm. Banks are generally open 8:30am–4pm Monday to Friday, and 9am– 1pm on Saturday, but some may not exchange money in the afternoons or on Saturdays. Post offices tend to open 9am–6pm, Monday to Friday, and 9am–1pm, Saturday. Small village branches may open only on weekday mornings.

Time Difference

In 2015, Quintana Roo state, which includes Cancún and the Riviera, changed time zones: it is now 5 hours behind GMT year-round. Yucatán and Campeche, which make up the rest of the Yucatán Peninsula, are 5 hours behind GMT in summer and six hours behind GMT in the winter.

Electrical Appliances

Electricity in Mexico operates on a 110-volt system, as in the US and Canada, and with the same American-type of flatpin plugs. For equipment using 220–240 volts, you will need transformers and plug adaptors.

Weather

The Yucatán has tropical weather, with a hot dry season from November to June, and a wet season from June to November. September to November is hurricane season. The peak seasons for vacation travel (and thus higher prices) are from mid-December to March, and July–August. The lowest prices are therefore to be found in May–June, and October–November.

Depending on term dates, in March and April the livelier resorts tend to be popular with young North American college students on spring break.

Sources of Information

There are well-staffed tourist offices in **Cancún**, **Mérida**, **Campeche**, **Playa del Carmen**, **Valladolid**, and **Isla Mujeres**. Useful online resources include **mexonline.com**, **riviera maya.com**, **cancun.com**,

and **cozumel.travel**. **Mexico Tourism** also has offices in the **U.K.**, **U.S.**, and **Canada**.

Travelers with Special Needs

Larger hotels and resorts in Cancún and Cozumel have good wheelchair facilities, but check before booking. Hotels in colonial buildings can be difficult to access, but sometimes have suitable first-floor rooms. Adapted bathrooms are being installed in official buildings, especially in Cancún and the main resorts, but they are rare elsewhere. Cancún sidewalks have wheelchair ramps at street junctions. Elsewhere you'll find dips in the sidewalk kerb.

Public transportation provision for the disabled is poor, although there are

wheelchair ramps and disabled toilets at Cancún Airport. Buses rarely have special provision for wheelchairs, but drivers are generally helpful.

The slow ferries to Isla Mujeres are easier to board than the fast, enclosed boats, and the crews are very helpful. For Cozumel, there is no choice but enclosed boats from Playa del Carmen, but staff can help.

Of the other attractions, eco-parks are generally the easiest to visit. Most Mayan sites have steps and narrow, stony paths, but larger sites, such as Chichén Itzá and Uxmal, have relatively smooth walkways. **Yucatek Divers** in Playa del Carmen has a program for disabled divers. **Access-Able, SATH** and **Mobility International USA** are useful resources.

DIRECTORY

POSTAL SERVICES

Mexpost
W correosdemexico.com

TV, RADIO, AND THE PRESS

Cancun Tips
W cancuntips.com

Diario de Yucatán
W yucatan.com.mx

Free Blue Guide
W thefreeblueguide.com

Mexico News Daily
W mexiconewsdaily.com

The Playa Times
W theplayatimes.com

Voice of America
W voanews.com

Yucatan Today
W yucatantoday.com

SOURCES OF INFORMATION

Campeche Tourist Office
Casa Seis, Parque Principal
W campeche.travel

Cancun.com
W cancun.travel/en/

Cancún Tourist Office
Cancún Town Hall,
Av Tulum

Isla Cozumel
W cozumel.travel

Isla Mujeres Tourist Office
Av Rueda Medina 130

Mérida Tourist Office
Calle 62, Centro Palacio Municipal

Mexico Tourism
W visitmexico.com

Mexico Tourism, Canada
C (416) 925 2753

Mexico Tourism, U.K.
C (44) 171 488 9392

Mexico Tourism, U.S.
C (212) 308 2110

Mexonline.com
W mexonline.com

Playa del Carmen Tourist Office
Av Juárez, corner of Av 15

Riviera Maya
W rivieramaya.com

Valladolid Tourist Office
Southeastern corner of town square
W valladolid.gob.mx/turismo

TRAVELERS WITH SPECIAL NEEDS

Access-Able
W access-able.com

Mobility International USA
W miusa.org

Society for Accessible Travel and Hospitality (SATH)
W sath.org

Yucatek Divers
Av 15 North,
between C/2 and 4,
Playa del Carmen
C (984) 803 2836
W yucatek-divers.com

Trips and Tours

Local travel agencies can be good for unusual tours, diving, forest trips, and so on. Among the best is **Mayan Heritage** in Mérida. Many companies offer guided tours to the main Mayan sites, but few allow more than an hour and a half on-site, and they often arrive all together at the hottest part of the day.

For simple city tours, Mérida's Paseo Turístico bus leaves from Parque Santa Lucía several times daily. In Campeche, the Tranvía de la Ciudad runs bus tours from the Parque Principal, and another bus, El Guapo, also has trips to the fortress-museums of San José and San Miguel.

Chichén Itzá, Uxmal, and Cobá have official guides, who can show you round for an hourly fee. Able linguists, they are often highly informative, though guides at smaller sites are less likely to be genuinely knowledgeable.

Agencies in the Sian Ka'an Biopshere Reserve (see pp26–7) offer some excellent day tours, and a number of companies, such as **Alltournative**, **Ecoturismo Yucatán**, and **Ecocolors**, specialize in nature and bird-watching trips. Fishermen in the Campeche Petenes (see p54) will be able to take you to places you'd never discover without local knowledge, while boatmen in Río Lagartos and Celestún (see p55) run trips to see the flamingos.

Most ecotours are run by small-scale operators, who can be hard to find. Essential resources include the websites of the **Yucatan Wildlife** and **Pronatura** organizations.

Dive shops abound on the Riviera, many of which also offer snorkeling trips, including **Aquatech**, **Almost Heaven**, **Phocéa Caribe**, **Yucatek Divers** (see p123), **Aqua World** (see p56), and **Squalo Adventures**. Several dive companies, such as the **Cenote Dive Center**, offer cenote tours, with diving or snorkeling, especially around Tulum.

Specialist fishing-trip agencies and fishing lodges get booked up far in advance. For casual fishing, the best places include Isla Mujeres, Cozumel, Isla Holbox, and Puerto Morelos.

For flights in a light aircraft, there's **Aerosaab** in Playa del Carmen and Isla Mujeres, or you could try a helicopter fight with **Cancún Helicopter**.

Shopping

The Riviera is a huge souvenir repository: you'll find whole malls dedicated to souvenir items in Cancún and Playa del Carmen. Mérida and Campeche have official handicrafts stores (casas de artesanías), which sell traditional crafts, though prices are a little higher than the norm.

Jewelry stores aimed at cruise passengers are a specialty of Cozumel and, to a lesser extent, Isla Mujeres and Cancún. As well as the bling, they sell items made with local jade, amber, and black obsidian. Playa del Carmen and Cancún have a number of stores showcasing quality silver work.

Fine embroidery of bright flower patterns on a plain white background is one of the foremost traditional products of the Yucatán, most often seen in the simple huípil blouses of Mayan women but also on items such as handkerchiefs and tablecloths. Valladolid and Mérida are the best places to find good embroidery.

Hammocks vary a lot in quality. The toughest ones are 100 per cent cotton. The specialist hammock shops in the market area in Mérida are the best places to look for one.

Panamas make great sunhats, and the best will regain their shape even after being rolled up for packing: head to Mérida market and the small specialist shops nearby.

For tequila, take advantage of the excellent duty-free selection at Cancún Airport. Cheaper and more local Yucatán specialties include fine rums and xtabentún, a sweet, herby, traditional Mayan honey drink.

Haggling is accepted in markets, especially for larger items, but it should not be intensive or drawnout. Many shops offer discounts if you buy more than one of any item.

Where to Eat

A restaurante will usually be more comfortable than a plastic-chaired lonchería (where you eat "lonch") or a cocina económica ("budget kitchen"), which offers diners good, simple local cooking.

Most waiters will not bring you the check/bill (la cuenta or la nota) until you ask for it. It's normal to tip – the usual rate is about 10 per cent; on the Riviera, waiters often expect 15 per cent. Some restaurants add a service charge – generally 10 per cent – to the bill.

On most restaurant tables you'll find two little bowls of sauce. The red one is relatively gentle; the green one, made with habanero chilis, blows the head off the uninitiated. Apart from this, Yucatecan dishes are more fragrant than spicy.

Mexicans snack constantly. Some dishes are small, others big platters of mixed fish, seafood, and salads. They enjoy *comida*, which is traditionally the largest meal of the day and is usually eaten in the afternoon. In every town and village, vendors offer tacos, *tortas* and other *antojitos* (see p69), ice cream and fruit.

The area has a great range of fresh fruits, such as mangoes, watermelon, and native *mamey* fruit. Juice shops serve it three ways: as straight juice; a *licuado*, blended with a little water or milk; or an *agua*, with water and ice.

Tequila comes from Jalisco, but is found across the Yucatán, and some bars specialize in tastings of the many labels. *Blanco* is the youngest tequila; *reposado* is aged for up to 11 months; darker *añejo* is aged for up to five years. Being largely exported, tequila has become fairly expensive in Mexico itself.

As well as international beer brands, the Yucatán has its own Montejo brewery, with a fine light beer (Montejo Especial) and a great ale, León Negra. Most restaurants have only a small choice of Mexican wines; upscale restaurants usually serve imported US, European, and Chilean wines, at very high prices. The *cantina* is the most traditional Mexican bar. There used to be laws barring women, and decreeing that nobody should be able to see in. You can still find old-style *cantinas* with secretive, screened doorways, but modern ones are actually quite comfortable.

Where to Stay

The region is home to a wide range of accommodations to suit all budgets, from luxury resorts and hip boutique hotels to family-run guesthouses and economical hostels. **Bookings.com**, **Hotels. com**, and **BestDay.com** are useful for bookings.

Cabañas (cabins), often with kitchens, are a good value, self-catering option for families and groups. Haciendas (colonial-era ranches) are a pricey, though atmospheric, choice. Another option is to stay in a private home or villa, booked through sites such as **Homestay.com**, **VRBO**, and **AirBnB**.

DIRECTORY

TRIPS AND TOURS

Aerosaab
☎ (998) 865 42 25
🖳 aerosaab.com

Almost Heaven Adventures, Puerto Morelos
☎ (998) 846 8009
🖳 almostheaven adventures.com

Alltournative, Playa del Carmen
☎ (984) 803 9999
🖳 alltournative.com

Aquatech-Villas de Rosa, Akumal
☎ (984) 875 9020
🖳 cenotes.com

Cancún Helicopter
☎ (998) 197 4324
🖳 cancunhelicopter.com

Cenote Dive Center, Tulum
☎ (984) 876 3285
🖳 cenotedive.com

Ecocolors, Cancún
☎ (998) 884 9580
🖳 ecotravelmexico.com

Ecoturismo Yucatán, Mérida
☎ (999) 920 2772
🖳 ecoyuc.com.mx

Mayan Heritage, Mérida
☎ (999) 924 9267
🖳 mayanheritage.com.mx

Phocéa Caribe, Playa del Carmen
☎ (984) 873 1210
🖳 phocea-mexico.com

Pronatura
☎ (555) 635 5054
🖳 pronatura.org.mx

Squalo Adventures, Isla Mujeres
☎ (998) 274 1644
🖳 squaloadventures.com

Yucatan Wildlife
☎ (998) 274 1644
🖳 yucatanwildlife.com

WHERE TO STAY

AirBnB
🖳 airbnb.com

BestDay.com
🖳 bestday.com

Bookings.com
🖳 bookings.com

Homestay.com
🖳 homestay.com

Hotels.com
🖳 hotels.com

VRBO
🖳 vrbo.com

Where to Stay

PRICE CATEGORIES

For a standard, double room per night (with breakfast if included), taxes, and extra charges.

$ under $60 $$ $60–$150 $$$ Over $150

Luxury Hotels

Casa de los Sueños, Isla Mujeres

MAP L2 ▪ Carretera Garrafón ▪ (998) 877 0651 ▪ www.casasuenos. com ▪ $$$

This secluded lodge is situated toward the southern end of Isla Mujeres. It has ten spacious rooms, a swimming pool, and oceanside terrace, all in contemporary Mexican style. It's stunning to look at and supremely comfortable.

Fiesta Americana, Mérida

MAP C2 ▪ Paseo de Montejo 451 ▪ (999) 942 1111 ▪ www.fiestameri cana.com ▪ $$$

Mérida's premier hotel is modern but built in an ornate French-mansion style, with a spectacular stained-glass atrium. Rooms are spacious and well-equipped.

Fiesta Americana Grand Coral Beach, Cancún

MAP L4 ▪ Blvd Kukulcán, km 9.5 ▪ (998) 881 3200 ▪ www.coralbeachcancun resort.com ▪ $$$

With cascades of greenery spilling down from its many balconies, the awesomely huge Coral Beach has 602 rooms and a thick catalog of facilities, including tennis courts and its own jogging track, as well as a private beach.

Hacienda Chichén, Chichén Itzá

MAP E3 ▪ (999) 920 8407 ▪ www.haciendachichen. com ▪ $$$

This place is set in an old colonial hacienda next to the site of Chichén Itzá. Most of the airy rooms are in bungalows used by archaeologists in the 1920s. It's now an award-winning eco-resort and spa, offering organic food and holistic treatments.

Hacienda Uxmal

MAP C4 ▪ (998) 887 2495 ▪ www.mayaland.com/ hacienda-uxmal ▪ $$$

This big hotel near the Uxmal site was built in the 1950s and has a gracious style extending through its colonial-style patios. The spacious, cool, and airy rooms have verandas and are decorated with characterful wooden furniture. The service is charming.

Hotel Secreto, Isla Mujeres

MAP L1 ▪ Playa Norte ▪ (998) 877 1039 ▪ www. hotelsecreto.com ▪ $$$

Hidden away on the far side of Isla Mujeres, this small hotel is utterly quiet, even though it is located just a few minutes' walk from the center of town. Furnished with four-poster beds, the nine suites overlook the Caribbean. The hotel also has a long pool and outdoor "living room" bar.

InterContinental Presidente, Cozumel

MAP R5 ▪ Carretera a Chankanaab, km 6.5 ▪ (1) 877 660 8550 ▪ www.intercontinental. com ▪ $$$

Big for Cozumel, but smallish by Cancún standards (218 rooms), this is one of the island's longest-established hotels. It enjoys a superb location with its own marina. Diving, snorkeling, and fishing trips can be arranged, but some sections of coral reef are within easy swimming distance of the hotel's long stretch of private, white-sand beachfront.

JW Marriott, Cancún

MAP K5 ▪ Blvd Kukulcán, km 14.5 ▪ (998) 848 9600 ▪ www.marriott.com ▪ $$$

This large hotel in Cancún is next door to the same company's slightly older Casa Magna. Expect state-of-the-art facilities, from the lavish health spa to the multitude of electronic accessories in the rooms.

Ritz Carlton, Cancún

MAP K5 ▪ Retorno del Rey 36 ▪ (998) 881 0808 ▪ www.ritzcarlton.com ▪ $$$

Top of the scale for sheer luxury in Cancún, the Ritz Carlton looks like the biggest, grandest Italian Renaissance palace ever built. All 365 rooms have ocean views, balconies, or terraces, and there's a private beach and five restaurants, plus a spa and a cookery school.

Zoëtry Villa Rolandi, Isla Mujeres
MAP L1/2 ▪ Fraccion-amiento Laguna Mar ▪ (998) 999 2000 ▪ www.zoetryresorts.com/mujeres ▪ $$$

A modest-sized hotel on the western side of Isla's Laguna Macax, with its own beach and boat landing stage, and superb views across to Cancún. No children under 13 are admitted – honeymoons are a specialty. Each balcony has its own Jacuzzi.

Haciendas and Hip Hotels

Hacienda Yaxcopoil, near Mérida
MAP C2 ▪ Yaxcopoil village ▪ (999) 900 1193 ▪ www.yaxcopoil.com ▪ $$

Once one of the region's biggest haciendas, sprawling over some 22,000 acres (8,900 ha), Yaxcopoil is an atmospheric place to spend the night. There is a casa principal (main house) filled with colonial-era art and furnishings, plus a chapel, a small Mayan museum, along with a delightful guesthouse with en-suite rooms.

Casa Azul, Mérida
MAP C2 ▪ Calle 60, No. 343 by 35 and 37 ▪ (999) 925 5016 ▪ www.casaazulhotel.com ▪ $$$

This colonial-era house, named for its rich blue hue, is an exclusive property decorated with period antiques throughout. Guests can experience luxurious amenities and the utmost privacy during their stay. Service is formal and warm.

The Diplomat Boutique Hotel, Mérida
MAP C2 ▪ Calle 78, No. 493A by 59 and 59A ▪ (999) 117 2972 ▪ www.thediplomatmerida.com ▪ $$$

This colonial-era boutique hotel, run by Canadian expats, has four spacious suites. The original tiles and carefully selected antiques, along with the decor, create an ambience of an earlier era. Knowledgeable and warm service.

Hacienda Puerta Campeche, Campeche
MAP A5 ▪ C/59, No. 71 ▪ (981) 816 7508 ▪ www.puertacampeche.com ▪ $$$

A set of 17th-century houses have been transformed into the area's most original hotel. Rooms and suites have satellite TV, and the place also boasts a restaurant, lounge bar, and pool.

Hacienda San José Cholul, near Mérida
MAP C2 ▪ 18 miles (29 km) E of Mérida ▪ (999) 924 1333 ▪ www.haciendasanjosecholul.com ▪ $$$

This 17th-century estate is one of several aristocratic haciendas now converted into hotels. Rooms are spacious, with colonial-style furniture. There's an outdoor spa and a swimming pool set in luxuriant grounds.

Hacienda Santa Rosa, near Mérida
MAP C2 ▪ (999) 923 1923 ▪ www.haciendasantarosa.com ▪ $$$

In an area unknown to most visitors, just west of the Mérida–Campeche road, is another hacienda hotel featuring just 11 rooms and suites. The lofty, colonial-style rooms are gorgeous, and some come complete with their own little garden. The gourmet restaurant, bar (located in the estate's old chapel), and pool are in perfect harmony.

Hacienda Temozón, near Uxmal
MAP C4 ▪ (999) 923 8089 ▪ www.haciendatemozon.com ▪ $$$

This hacienda is the most luxurious place to stay near Uxmal, 27 miles (43 km) north of the site. The 17th-century main house, terrace restaurant, and pool are spectacular.

Hacienda Uayamón, Campeche
MAP A5 ▪ (981) 813 0530 ▪ www.haciendauayamon.com ▪ $$$

This is the most isolated of all the Plan haciendas, situated on a former henequen (sisal, used for ropemaking) plantation. The conversion has been done with style, and the swimming pool – set in a ruined, roofless building – is astonishing.

Hacienda Xcanatún, near Mérida
MAP C2 ▪ Xcanatún, 7 miles (12 km) N of Mérida ▪ (999) 930 2140 ▪ www.xcanatun.com ▪ $$$

This lovely 18th-century hacienda, five minutes from Mérida, offers 18 suites, each with a terrace and Jacuzzi, in luxuriant gardens. There's a terrace bar, two pools, a spa, and a superb restaurant, the Casa de Piedra, or Stone House (see p71).

Maroma Resort & Spa, Punta Maroma

MAP R4 ▪ (998) 872 8200 ▪ www.belmond.com/maroma-resort-and-spa-riviera-maya ▪ $$$

This opulent retreat is frequented by celebrities attracted to its 200 acres (81 ha) of lush jungle and stretch of private beach. Rooms are vast, and there are three superb pools as well as a choice of restaurants and bars. Honeymooners and beauty-therapy addicts are well catered for.

Resort Hotels

Akumal Bay Beach & Wellness Resort, Akumal

MAP P5 ▪ (984) 875 7500 ▪ www.akumalbayresort.com ▪ $$$

This medium-sized resort features an exquisite, large pool that snakes along beside some of the rooms. It's only a short walk from Akumal village along the beach, so those who appreciate the convenience of staying at an all-inclusive resort can also get a taste of local life whenever they wish.

Barceló Maya Beach Resort, Puerto Aventuras

MAP Q5 ▪ (984) 875 1500 ▪ www.barcelo.com ▪ $$$

This giant complex is made up of four hotels – the Beach, the Colonial, the Tropical, and the Caribe. They share over a mile (2 km) of beach and offer a range of on-site options at all-inclusive rates. The idea is that you "stay at one, play at four." Highlights include a nightclub under a giant *palapa*

plant and a luxurious beachside buffet.

Club Med Cancún

MAP K6 ▪ Punta Nizuc, Blvd Kukulcán, km 20 ▪ (998) 881 8200 ▪ www.clubmed.com ▪ $$$

This spacious site has the typical Club Med range of sports facilities – enough even when the 456 rooms fill up – and offers youth-oriented entertainment including a techno disco.

Grand Oasis, Cancún

MAP K5 ▪ Blvd Kukulcán, km 16.5 ▪ (998) 881 7000 ▪ www.oasishoteles.com ▪ $$$

Boasting 1,316 rooms, this hotel-resort is built on a grand scale. Three giant pyramids make up the main buildings. There are 16 restaurants and bars, and the Up & Down nightclub. The resort's swimming pool is one of Latin America's biggest. A vast range of water-sports and theme parties completes the picture.

Iberostar Cozumel

MAP R6 ▪ (987) 872 9900 ▪ www.iberostar.com ▪ $$$

The 300-room Iberostar faces an especially fine beach and is well located for diving and snorkeling in the west corner of the island, near Punta Francesa. Like the Tucán (see p130), it offers a wide range of activities.

Marina and Spa El Cid Riviera Maya, Puerto Morelos

MAP R3 ▪ Blvd El Cid Unidad 15, Puerto Morelos ▪ (998) 872 8999 ▪ www.elcid.com ▪ $$$

Set right on the ocean, this hotel combines

colonial and modern architecture. Guests can go snorkeling at the Puerto Morelos National Reef Park in front of the hotel.

Moon Palace Golf & Spa Resort, near Cancún

MAP R3 ▪ (998) 881 6000 ▪ www.moonpalacecancun.com ▪ $$$

The biggest all-inclusive resort of them all, with 2,131 luxurious rooms in beach-house style. It offers every possible activity, 14 restaurants, and a 27-hole golf course. It even regularly hosts major music and theatrical acts, including Cirque Du Soleil.

Reef Resort, Playacar

MAP Q4 ▪ Av Xaman Ha, Playacar ▪ (984) 873 4120 ▪ www.thereefplayacar.com ▪ $$$

A good-value spot compared to most places, offering an all-meals-included plan. Rooms and food are relatively basic, but it has a great beach location and a fine pool. Its simple style and all inslusive meals have won it many fans.

Royal Hideaway, Playa del Carmen

MAP Q4 ▪ Lote 6, Playacar ▪ (984) 873 4500 ▪ www.occidentalhotels.com ▪ $$$

This all-inclusive, adults-only resort prides itself on its excellent food, with a tempting choice of gourmet Spanish, Asian, and also Italian restaurants. The rooms come with ceiling fans, wicker furniture, and wood porches.

Secrets Capri Riviera Cancun, Playa del Carmen

MAP Q4 ▪ Carretera Federal 387, km 299 ▪ (984) 873 4880 ▪ www. secretsresorts.com/capri ▪ $$$

Only a few minutes north of Playa del Carmen, this adults-only all-inclusive resort still feels secluded, thanks to its setting in 70 acres (28 ha) of tropical oceanfront grounds. It has five excellent à la carte restaurants, an indulgent spa, and a beautiful beach.

Cabaña Hotels

Cabañas Costa del Sol, Punta Allen

MAP G5 ▪ Carretera Tulum, km. 57.5 ▪ (984) 876 9395 ▪ $

Five beachside bunga-lows located inside the biosphere reserve make a brilliant base for exploring this side of the Yucatán peninsula.

Coco's Cabañas, Punta Bete

MAP R4 ▪ Xcalacoco, Lte 2 ▪ (998) 874 7056 ▪ www.cocoscabanas. com ▪ $

Experience exceptional service at this simple property, with six cozy bungalows. There's a popular on-site restaurant that gets rave reviews.

Cabañas Paamul, Playa del Carmen

MAP Q4 ▪ (984) 875 1053 ▪ www.paamul.com ▪ $$

Spacious beach rooms amid a camp site; some are in a modern building, others in palm-roofed huts. There's an enjoyable bar-restaurant (see p98), and the uncrowded beach is exquisite.

Genesis Retreat, Ek-Balam

MAP F2 ▪ Off the NE corner of the town plaza ▪ (985) 100 4805 ▪ www. genesis retreat.com ▪ $$

A beautiful eco-lodge, Genesis is a lush garden set around a bio-filtered pool, with rooms tucked away in the greenery. Bird-watching trips and tours to meet the Mayan neighbors are offered. Food is sourced from a local organic farm.

Xamach Dos, Boca Paila

MAP G4 ▪ Beach Road, km 32 ▪ (719) 602 9414 ▪ www.xamachdos.com ▪ $$

This rustic, eco-friendly property features six unique *casitas* (wooden cabins). Its seaside location guarantees amazing views and there is a beautiful open-air restaurant.

Cabañas María del Mar, Isla Mujeres

MAP S1 ▪ Av Carlos Lazo 1 ▪ (998) 877 0179 ▪ www.cabanasdelmar. com ▪ $$$

A little island of mellow comfort just behind Isla's Playa Norte, with the most popular bar on the beach, Buho's, attached. There's a main building with rooms or cabaña-bungalows; some are on the small side, but they are all attractive. Health treatments and massages are a specialty.

Eco-Paraíso Xixim, near Celestún

MAP A3 ▪ (988) 916 2100, (55) 55 68 8246 ▪ www.hotelxixim.com ▪ $$$

This eco-retreat stands between coconut groves and a remote beach north of Celestún and is best accessed by four-wheel drive. Nature and archaeological guided tours are a specialty, and all cabins have beach terraces.

Mahekal Beach, Playa del Carmen

MAP Q4 ▪ C/38 Norte by 5th Av ▪ (984) 873 0579 US & Canada (1) 877 235 4452 ▪ www.mahekalbeach resort.com ▪ $$$

This is the ultimate in cabaña luxury: palm-roofed beach lodges with traditional Mexican fittings and five-star comforts. The pent-houses in particular are superb.

Papaya Playa, Tulum

MAP G4 ▪ Tulum Boca Paila, km 4.5 ▪ (1) 984 182 7389 ▪ www. papayaplaya.com ▪ $$$

This long-established cabaña hotel offers everything from a basic sand-floor cabin with a shared bathroom to private villas big enough for a family. Strung out along a wide stretch of uncrowded beach, most of the 80 cabañas have views directly onto the Caribbean Sea.

Rancho Sak Ol, Puerto Morelos

MAP R3 ▪ (998) 871 0181 ▪ www.ranchosakol.com ▪ $$$

Equipped with their trademark "hanging beds" – solid beds on ropes that swing – the cabins have a typical beachcomber look. The use of an open kitchen is included, and yoga is offered.

For a key to hotel price categories see p126

Mid-Range Hotels on the Riviera

Amaité Hotel & Spa, Isla Holbox

MAP G1 ■ C/Juárez, on the beach ■ (984) 875 2217 ■ www.amaitehotel holbox.com ■ $$

Just two blocks away from the main street, this hotel offers 15 comfortable rooms. The Mexican-style rooms are a real pleasure: the doubles and twins upstairs have balconies; the suites below have kitchenettes and terraces. There's a great restaurant, too.

Casa Tucán, Playa del Carmen

MAP Q4 ■ C/4, between Av 10 and Av 15 ■ (984) 873 0283 ■ www.casa tucan.de ■ $$

Casa Tucán seems small from the street, but within it is a maze of gardens, patios, and spiral staircases, leading to a leaf-shaded pool. All of the 30 rooms are cozy and colorful – some are palm-roofed cabañas; others are studios with a small kitchen. The friendly German owners offer dive packages arranged with the Yucatek Divers school (see p123).

Hotel Flamingo, Cozumel

MAP R5 ■ Calle 6 N, No. 81 ■ (987) 872 1264 ■ www.hotelflamingo. com ■ $$

Hotel Flamingo began as a dive hotel and still offers a good range of packages for divers. Even if you're not a scuba nut, it's a comfortable place, with well-cared-for rooms and a bar and rooftop sundeck and lounge.

Ibis Cancún Centro, Cancún

MAP K5 ■ Av Tulum s/n ■ (998) 272 8500 ■ www. ibis.com ■ $$

The Cancún branch of the international chain wins no prizes for character or charm, but is a solid, good-value choice amid a sea of overpriced mid-range options. The en-suites are clean and comfortable, the staff are efficient, and the hotel's downtown location is convenient for transport connections (including the airport). There is a mini-supermarket next to the hotel entrance.

Mom's Hotel, Playa del Carmen

MAP Q4 ■ Av 30, by C/4 ■ (984) 873 0315 ■ www. momshotel.com ■ $$

Texan Ricco Merkle's long-running hotel is, as its name suggests, a welcoming home-from-home. The rooms have been going a few years but are comfortable and pretty, and there's a tiny pool in the courtyard, plus a rooftop bar that's a great place for meeting up with people.

Plaza Caribe, Cancún

MAP J3 ■ Av Tulum 19, corner of Av Uxmal ■ (998) 884 1377 ■ www.hotelplazacaribe. patios, com ■ $$

This large hotel's main selling point is that it is right opposite the bus station in Ciudad Cancún, and so is always popular. Despite being in such a traffic-heavy area, it's surprisingly peaceful inside, with attractive and comfortable rooms, pretty gardens, a pleasant pool, a gym, and dining on-site.

Villa Kiin, Isla Mujeres

MAP L1 ■ C/Zazil-Ha, No. 129, Playa Norte ■ (998) 877 1024 ■ www. villakiin.com ■ $$

All the rooms here are different – some are on the beach, some are like separate little beach houses – but all are comfortable and furnished with attractive Mexican textiles. Villa Kiin is in a delightful location, facing the placid Playa Secreto lagoon; snorkel gear is available for guests' use.

Piedra Escondida, Tulum

MAP P6 ■ Tulum Ruinas, Boca Paila Rd, km 3.5 ■ (984) 100 1443 ■ www. piedraescondida.com ■ $$$

Eight rooms, in two-story cabaña-style beach huts, all come with decent showers and entrancing views. The restaurant serves a range of Italian and Mexican food.

Tankah Dive Inn, Tankah

MAP P6 ■ Bahía Tankah No. 16, Tulum ■ (984) 100 1512 ■ www.tankah.com ■ $$$

This laid-back hotel on the Riviera has only a few rooms, but they're all comfortable and full of character. Diving is a big attraction, of course, but it's okay just to sit on the beach and sample the fine cuisine.

Villas de Rosa Beach Resort, Akumal

MAP P5 ■ Carrt. Puerto Aventuras–Akuma, km 115 ■ (984) 875 9020 ■ www.cenotes.com ■ $$$

Owners Nancy and Tony de Rosa are the foremost

Where to Stay « **131**

cave-diving specialists on the Riviera, and many of their guests come here to dive. The hotel is also well equipped for families.

Mid-Range Hotels Elsewhere

Casa Hamaca, Valladolid

MAP E3 ■ Parque San Juan, C/49, No. 202A at C/40 ■ (985) 100 4272 ■ www.casahamaca.com ■ $$

This large guesthouse, with its delightful, tree-shaded garden, has a countryside feel. It offers not just comfortable beds, but also full spa services and healthy breakfasts.

Eclipse, Mérida

MAP C2 ■ Calle 57, No. 491 ■ (999) 923 1600 ■ www.hoteleclipse merida.com.mx ■ $$

In contrast to most hotels in the city, the Eclipse is strikingly modern. Its rooms are bright and breezy, and each one has a themed mural (Andy Warhol, Las Vegas, Zen, and Cinema are among the styles). There's a small swimming pool, and the location is convenient for the city's main attractions.

Ecotel Quinta Regia, Valladolid

MAP E3 ■ C/40, No. 160A, between C/27 and C/29 ■ (985) 856 3476 ■ www.ecotelquintaregia.com.mx ■ $$

Built in a neo-colonial style, this hotel combines a colorful Mexican look with modern facilities. Lush gardens are overlooked by the best rooms. The pool is secluded, and the restaurant makes use of seasonal garden produce.

El Marqués, Valladolid

MAP E3 ■ C/39, No. 203, on Parque Principal ■ (985) 856 2073 ■ www.mesondelmarques.com ■ $$

Valladolid's classic hotel occupies one of its finest old colonial houses, with rooms set around several flower-filled, elegant patios. There's a great restaurant (see p107) and a pool.

Hacienda Uxmal, Uxmal

MAP C4 ■ (997) 976 2040 ■ www.mayaland.com ■ $$

This hacienda is part of a small chain of hotels located at some of the ancient Mayan sites. All are built in old-Mexican, hacienda style, complete with charming rooms and lush and well-tended gardens. The Uxmal branch offers exceptional value for money.

Hotel Baluartes, Campeche

MAP A5 ■ Av 16 de Septiembre 128 ■ (981) 816 3911 ■ www.baluartes.com.mx ■ $$

Campeche has only a limited selection of hotels. This lofty 1970s building on the seafront is more comfortable than most. Be sure to ask for a room with a sea view to catch the magnificent sunsets over the Gulf of Mexico.

Hotel Dolores Alba, Chichén Itzá

MAP E3 ■ Hwy 180, 2 miles (3 km) E of Chichén Itzá ■ (985) 858 1555 ■ www.doloresalba.com ■ $$

The best-value place to stay near Chichén, this roadside hotel has

40 bright and comfortable bungalow rooms, a restaurant, and two pools. Mérida has a sister hotel of the same name – don't confuse the two when booking your stay.

Hotel Marionetas, Mérida

MAP C2 ■ C/49, No. 516, between C/62 & C/64 ■ (999) 928 3377 ■ www.hotelmarionetas.com ■ $$

Once a puppet theater, the colonial building that forms the core of this hotel has been beautifully restored with rooms painted in pastel shades with rustic ceramics. The hotel has a large pool, and helpful staff serve a delicious breakfast.

Hotel San Felipe, San Felipe

MAP E1 ■ C/9, between C/14 and C/16 ■ (986) 862 2027 ■ $$

Staying near Río Lagartos used to be a problem, so this hotel is a welcome arrival. The waterside restaurant serves the catch of the day, and all the spacious rooms have sitting areas. Ask for a lagoon-view balcony.

La Misión de Fray Diego, Mérida

MAP C2 ■ C/61, No. 524, between C/64 and C/66 ■ (999) 924 1111 ■ www.lamisiondefraydiego.com ■ $$

This grand 17th-century former monastery has been lavishly converted with a mix of antiques and all-modern bathrooms, a pool, and other services. Some rooms have a real Spanish-mansion air; others are a little less exciting, and prices will vary accordingly.

For a key to hotel price categories see p126

Guesthouses and B&Bs

Amar Inn, Puerto Morelos

MAP R3 ■ Av Rojo Gómez ■ (998) 871 0026 ■ $$
This seafront B&B has lovely views and offers its guests a delightfully rustic atmosphere. The decor is very traditional and each room has been painted a different color. The inn can arrange tours to nearby tourist spots. This is just the right place for travelers looking for a welcoming and homey spot typical of the region.

Amigo's Hostel, Cozumel

MAP R5 ■ Calle 7 Sur, No. 571, between Av 30 and 25, Centro, Cozumel ■ (987) 872 3868 ■ www. cozumelhostel.com ■ $$
This hostel offers two large mixed dormitories and one private room with a kitchenette and private terrace, all set around a pool and lovely garden. The place is especially suited to family groups: breakfasts are included and are served in a garden *palapa* or a palm-roofed gazebo.

Casa del Maya B&B, Mérida

MAP C2 ■ C/66, No. 410A, between C/45 and C/47 Centro ■ (1) 999 181 1880 ■ www. casadelmaya.com ■ $$
Once the home of an old Mérida family, this 19th-century house has been delightfully restored with six charming, lofty-ceilinged rooms. There's a lovely garden and pool, and breakfast on the terrace includes home-baked cinnamon rolls.

Casa Mexilio, Mérida

MAP C2 ■ C/68, No. 495, between C/59 and C/57 ■ (999) 928 2505 ■ www. casamexilio.com ■ $$
This is a very special guesthouse in a fine old building. The hallways and eight rooms have traditional furniture and antiques, including some four-poster beds, and the Mexican-American owners have added many original touches, including a magical, fern-bedecked swimming pool.

Flycatcher Inn, Santa Elena

Calle 20, off Hwy-261 ■ (997) 978 5350 ■ www. flycatcherinn.com ■ $$
This pretty little B&B is decorated with locally made furniture and wall hangings. The owners are very knowledgeable about the archaeological sites located nearby.

Julamis, Mérida

MAP C2 ■ Calle 53, No. 475B ■ (999) 924 1818 ■ www.hoteljulamis.com ■ $$
Award-winning, adults-only guesthouse based in a charming colonial-era building lovingly restored by its Cuban owners. Each of the nine immaculate rooms has been decorated in a different style, but all are elegant and comfortable. Mini-fridges stocked with free beer, water, and soft drinks are a nice touch.

Luz en Yucatán, Mérida

MAP C2 ■ C/55, No. 499, between C/58 and C/60 ■ (999) 924 0035 ■ www. luzenyucatán.com ■ $$
Once part of a convent, this house is now a quirky and charming urban retreat featuring a lovely pool and modern apartments at bargain prices.

Macanché, Izamal

MAP D2 ■ C/22, No. 305, between C/33 and C/35 ■ (988) 954 0287 ■ www. macanche.com ■ $$
Izamal is a tranquil town in any case, but the pretty walled garden, within which hides this B&B, is especially soothing. The lttle bungalows are dotted about the garden, each imaginatively decorated; one has a kitchen.

Posada Sirena, Punta Allen

MAP G5 ■ Fax (984) 139 1241 ■ www.casasirena. com ■ $$
Punta Allen is about the most beachcomberish destination imaginable, and this guesthouse hits the appropriate note, with a stay-as-long-as-you-want feel from owner Serena, a real character. The four cabins each have their own kitchen and the obligatory hammocks. She can also arrange fishing and diving trips.

Tamarindo, Cozumel

MAP R5 ■ Calle 4 Norte, No. 421, between 20 and 25 ■ (987) 872 3614 ■ www.tamarindobedand breakfast.com ■ $$
A stylish property, with a sheltered garden, run by Mexican-French owners. Each of the five pretty rooms has its own character, there's an open kitchen and ample breakfasts, and they have many happy clients. They also run Palapas Amaranto nearby, which offers self-contained suites ideal for families or friends.

Budget Accommodations

Albergue La Candelaria, Valladolid

MAP E3 ▪ C/35, No. 201F, between C/42 and C/44 ▪ (985) 856 2267 ▪ www.hostelvalladolidyucatan.com ▪ $

This hostel, set in a pretty, old house offers excellent, bright dormitory rooms, and shared bathrooms, and a generous breakfast. There's also a lounge and a hammock-strung garden for the use of guests.

Hostel Quetzal, Cancún

MAP J3 ▪ Orquideas 10, Mz 14 ▪ (998) 883 9821 ▪ www.hostelquetzal.com ▪ $

Centrally located, this popular hostel offers both private and dormitory-style rooms with air-conditioning, and some with en-suite bathrooms. Breakfast and dinner are included and there are nightly cocktail parties.

Hotel Carmelina, Isla Mujeres

MAP L1 ▪ Isla Town, between Av Abasolo and Av Guerrero ▪ (998) 877 0006 ▪ $

This laid-back place has been welcoming budget travelers for years. Set around a big patio, its rooms are simple and cheerful. All have showers, air-conditioning, ceiling fans, and mini-fridges.

Hotel Pepita, Cozumel

MAP R5 ▪ Av 15A Sur, No. 120 ▪ (987) 872 0098 ▪ www.hotelpepitacozumel.com ▪ $

Friendly, helpful owners make the difference in this big, popular hotel. Rooms are well cared for and have such extras as air-conditioning and small fridges. Complimentary coffee is provided.

Nómadas Hostel, Mérida

MAP C2 ▪ C/62, No. 433, by C/51 ▪ (999) 924 5223 ▪ www.nomadastravel.com ▪ $

Challenging the cheap hotels of Mérida for value, this hostel has bright, airy dorm rooms as well as 20 private doubles. There's also an open kitchen, a lounge space, and cheap Internet access.

Tribu Hostel, Isla Holbox

MAP G1 ▪ Av Pedro Joaquin Coldwell s/n ▪ (984) 875 2507 ▪ www.tribuhostel.com ▪ $

One of the best hostels in the region, Tribu has well-maintained dorms and private rooms, as well as a hammock-strewn garden, roof terrace, lively bar, and kitchen for guests to use. Movie nights, barbecues, salsa dances, Spanish classes, yoga, and kite-surfing are among the many activities on offer here.

Hotel Casa del Balam, Mérida

MAP C2 ▪ Calle 60, No. 468 ▪ (999) 924 8844 ▪ www.casadelbalam.com ▪ $$

One of the oldest hotels in Mérida, Casa del Balam, retains its erstwhile charm, thanks, in part, to its tranquil courtyard. Rooms are spacious with air-conditioning and bright decor. There's a good on-site restaurant, and the hotel is also located nearby major sights of Centro. Guests can enjoy a homely ambience and attentive service.

Hotel Rinconada del Convento, Izamal

MAP D2 ▪ Calle 33, No. 294 ▪ (988) 954 0151 ▪ www.cabanascopal.com ▪ $$

This centrally located hotel is within walking distance of major attractions and restaurants. Rooms have minimal decor and are furnished with basic necessities, making this a good base for those wanting to get out and explore. Some rooms offer views. Guests can relax in the garden or enjoy themselves at the pool.

Popol Vuh, Playa del Carmen

MAP Q4 ▪ C/2, between Av 5 and the beach ▪ No air-con in some rooms; no en-suite ▪ (984) 803 2149 ▪ $$

A remarkable survivor from Playa's hippy days, clinging on to its great beach location in the face of glossier developments. Set inside two garden enclosures are simple cabañas (with or without showers), a private room, and a shared dormitory.

Posada Amor, Puerto Morelos

MAP R3 ▪ On the plaza ▪ (998) 871 0033 ▪ No air-con in some rooms ▪ posada-amor.wix.com/puertom ▪ $$

Featuring Puerto Morelos' best low-priced rooms, Posada Amor has a friendly feel and popular restaurant. The rooms come in a range of shapes and sizes.

For a key to hotel price categories see p126

Index

Page numbers in **bold** refer to main entries.

Acknowledgments

Author Nick Rider is a freelance travel writer and editor, based in London **Additional contributor** Shafik Meghji **Publishing Director** Georgina Dee. **Publisher** Vivien Antwi. **Design Director** Phil Ormerod. **Editorial** Ankita Awasthi Tröger, Michelle Crane, Dipika Dasgupta, Rachel Fox, Fay Franklin, Freddie Marriage, Lucy Richards, Sally Schafer **Design** Tessa Bindloss, Richard Czapnik, Bharti Karakoti, Rahul Kumar, Bhavika Mathur, Priyanka Thakur, Stuti Tiwari, Vinita Venugopal **Picture Research** Susie Peachey, Ellen Root, Lucy Sienkowska, Oran Tarjan **Commissioned Photography** Demetrio Carrasco, Linda Whitwam **Cartography** Tom Coulson, Martin Darlison, Suresh Kumar, Casper Morris, Animesh Kumar Pathak **DTP** Jason Little **Production** Luca Bazzoli **Factchecker** Julie Schwietert Collazo **Proofreader** Clare Peel **Indexer** Helen Peters

First edition created by Blue Island Publishing.

Picture Credits
The publisher would like to thank the following for their kind permission to reproduce their photographs:
Key: a-above; b-below/bottom; c-centre; f-far; l-left; r-right; t-top
123RF.com: Franck Camhi 107cra; macmonican 103clb; manganganath 82cl; Borna Mirahmadian 74b. **Alamy Stock Photo:** age fotostock / Blaine Harrington 17tl, 57b, 62bl, / Cem Canbay 88-9. / Gonzalo Azumendi 7tr, / Jordi Cami 3tl, 76-7. / Leonardo Díaz Romero 102cb, all 51b; The Art Archive / Gianni Dagli Orti 36cl, 48ca; Danita Delimont / Julie Eggers 105tr, 111cla, 112tr; Reinhard Dirscherl 22bl; Michael Dwyer 43br; John Elk III 4crb; Robert Fried 27crb; Eddy Galeotti 109b; Nicholas Gill 70br; Granger Historical Picture Archive 31b, 42br, 43tl, 31b; Hugh Hargrave 4t; hemis.fr / Gil Giuglio 72tl, / Paule Seux 46b; Marshall Ikonography 36bc, 73tr, 100tl; imageBROKER / Vision 21 21cr; incamerastock 15tc; Brian Jannsen 22-3; Konstantin Kalishko 38-9; Larry Larsen 64cl; Melvyn Longhurst 33tr; Alain Machet (3) 10cr; Richard Maschmeyer 24-5; Michael DeFreitas Central America 65b, 91cr; John Mitchell 12cl, 32br; Mostardi Photography 37cr; Eric Nathan 15bl; NatureWorld 4cl; Brian Overcast 32ca, 61crb; George Oze 56tr; Stefano Paterna 113c; Pictures Colour Library 11cra; Chuck Place 42cl; robertharding / Michael DeFreitas 90tl; Grant Rooney 84b; David Sanger Photography 1; Fedor Selivanov 4cla; Septemberlegs 110cla, 110br; Witold Skrypczak 72br, 101cb, 104b; David South 31cr, 38cr, 49crb; Johnny Stockshooter 2tr, 40-1; Topcris 80tl; Ken Welsh 35tc; Andrew Woodley 98cla; Ariadne Van Zandbergen 11c. **Alux Restaurant & Lounge:** 86cla. **Aqua World:** 56cl. **Azul Gallery:** 96tc. **Carlos 'n Charlie's:** 66b, 97tr. **Casa de Piedra:** 115cr. **Casa Denis:** 99clb. **Dady'O:** Carlos Garcia Carrillo 67tr. **Dreamstime.com:** Agcuesta 73br; Jean-luc Azou 37b, 38cl, 54c; Yulia Belousova 28cla; Florian Blümm 44-5; Flavia Campos 71tr; Salvador Ceja 4b, 29c; Rafal Cichawa 34-5; Sorin Colac 28-9; Maciej Czekajewski 54tl; Czuber 67b, 106clb; Eddygaleotti 3tr, 29tl, 38br, 46tl, 83t, 116-7; Eutoch 79t; Vlad Ghiea 6cl, Richard Gunion 69cla; Inishka777 10clb, 14-5, 16-7, 50cr; Javarman 12-3; Karlos4kintero 10bl; James Kelley 53br; Patryk Kosmider 16bl; Kravka 7br; Jesús Eloy Ramos Lara 11crb, 11bl, 48b; Lev Levin 23cr; Lucagal 101br; Lunamarina 20br, 20-1, 30tr, 50clb, 68tl; Danilo Mongiello 23tl, Thiago Henrique Neves 80-1; Olga Nosova 92tl; Piotr Pawinski 105c; Boris Philchev 102t; Seaphotoart 52tl, 92b; Siempreverde22 2tl, 8-9; Jo Ann Snover 108tl, Softlightaa 34bl, Jose I. Soto 17cr; stockcreations 69br; Jennifer Stone 75tr; Alyaksandr Stzhalkouski 13tl; Subbotina 20clb; Barna Tanko 29cr, 112bl; Slobodan Tomic 35cr; Peter Zaharov 58cl; Suriel Ramirez Zaldivar 68crb. **Evolution Music Inc./Cancun Jazz Festival:** 14cl, 55cr. **Experiencias Xcaret:** 18t, 18c, 19bl, 78tl, 81cla; Park / Erik Ruiz 19cr. **FLPA:** Minden Pictures / Donald M. Jones 11tl, 27cra, / Pete Oxford 26bl. **Getty Images:** Tony Anderson 73cl; Witold Skrypczak 26-7, 47tl, Dallas Stribley 60b. **Conacuta-INAH-MEX:** Authorized reproduction by the Instituto Nacional de Antropología e Historia 45cl. **La Chaya Maya:** 71l. **La Parrilla:** 87bl. **Grupo Mandala:** Palazzo 85cla. **Moon Palace:** 82br. **MUSA:** Elier Amado Gil / The Stills LifeStyle Agency / Gino Caballero 4cr, 12br. **Photoshot:** Mahaux Charles 109tr; Frank Fell 10cla, Wolfgang Kaehler 96bl; Victor Korchenko 63cl; World Pictures / Stuart Pearce 49tl. **Piedra de Agua Hotel Boutique:** RolloDigital2014 114cra. **Robert Harding Picture Library:** Michael DeFreitas 14cl, 55cr. **Señor Frog's:** Stanly photo 66cl. **SuperStock:** age fotostock 45tr, 63tr, / Blaine Harrington 6tr, 65cr, 94clb., / Cem Canbay 10crb, / Jan Wlodarczyk 30cl, / Jeff Greenberg 75cl, / Richard Maschmeyer 44cl, 101tl; Luis Javier Sandoval Alvarado 53cl; F1 ONLINE 59tr; Franz Marc Frei 55tl; Hemis.fr 79cl; imageBROKER / Katja Kreder 95br; LOOK-foto 52b, 62t; Minden Pictures / Pete Oxford 4clb; Photononstop 59b; Travel Library Limited 51tr, Travel Pictures Ltd 60tl. **Cover** Front and spine: **AWL Images:** Matteo Colombo. Back: **Dreamstime.com:** Sorincolac. **Pull Out Map Cover AWL Images:** Matteo Colombo.

All other images: © Dorling Kindersley
For further information see: www.dkimages.com

Penguin Random House

Printed and bound in China
First publishing in Great Britain in 2003
by Dorling Kindersley Limited
80 Strand, London WC2R 0RL
Copyright 2003, 2017 © Dorling Kindersley Limited
A Penguin Random House Company

17 18 19 20 10 9 8 7 6 5 4 3 2 1

Reprinted with revisions 2005, 2007, 2009, 2011, 2013, 2015, 2017

MIX
Paper from
responsible sources
FSC™ C018179

As a guide to abbreviations in visitor information blocks:
Adm = admission charge; **DA** = disabled access;
D = dinner; **L** = lunch.

Phrase Book

In an Emergency

Help!	¡Socorro!	soh-**koh**-roh
	Auxilio	o-xe-leo
Stop!	¡Pare!	pah-reh
Call a doctor!	¡Llame a un	yah-meh ah oon
	médico!	meh-dee-koh
Call an	¡Llame una	yah-meh ah
ambulance!	ambulancia!	oonah ahm-boo-lahn-see-ah
Call the fire	¡Llame a los	yah-meh ah lohs
department!	bomberos!	bohm-**beh**-rohs
Police!	policía!	poh-lee-**see**-ah

Communication Essentials

Yes	Sí	see
No	No	noh
Please	Por favor	pohr fah-**vohr**
Thank you	Gracias	**grah**-see-ahs
Excuse me	Perdone	pehr-**doh**-neh
Hello	Hola	oh-lah
Bye (casual)	Chau	chau
Goodbye	Adiós	ah-dee-**ohs**
What?	¿Qué?	keh
When?	¿Cuándo?	**kwahn**-doh
Why?	¿Por qué?	pohr-keh
Where?	¿Dónde?	**dohn**-deh
How are you?	¿Cómo está usted?	**koh**-moh ehs-**tah** oos-tehd
Very well, thank you	Muy bien, gracias	mwee-**behn grah**-see-ahs
Pleased to meet you	Mucho gusto	**moo**-choh **goo**-stoh
See you soon	Hasta pronto	ahs-tah **prohn**-toh
I'm sorry	Lo siento	loh see-**ehn**-toh

Useful Phrases

That's fine	Está bien	ehs-**tah** bee-**ehn**
Great/fantastic!	¡Qué bien!	keh bee-**ehn**
Where is/are…?	¿Dónde está/están…?	**dohn**-deh ehs-**tah**/ehs-**tahn**
How far is it to…?	¿Cuántos metros/ kilómetros hay de aquí a…?	**kwahn**-tohs **meh**-trohs/ kee-**loh**-meh-trohs eye deh ah-**kee** ah
Which way is it to…?	¿Por dónde se va a…?	pohr **dohn**-deh seh **vah** ah
Do you speak English?	¿Habla inglés?	**ah**-blah een-**glehs**
I don't understand	No comprendo/ entiendo	noh kohm-**prehn**-doh
I would like	Quisiera/ Me gustaría	kee-see-**yehr**-ah/ meh goo-**stah**-ree ah

Useful Words

big	grande	**grahn**-deh
small	pequeño/a	peh-**keh**-nyoh/ nyah
hot	caliente	kah-lee-**ehn**-teh
cold	frío/a	**free**-oh/ah
good	bueno/a	**bweh**-noh/nah
bad	malo/a	**mah**-loh/lah
open	abierto/a	ah-bee-**ehr**-toh/tah
closed	cerrado/a	sehr-**rah**-doh/ dah
full	lleno/a	**yeh**-noh/nah
empty	vacío/a	vah-**see**-oh/ah
left	izquierda	ees-key-**ehr**-dah
right	derecha	deh-**reh**-chah
(keep) straight ahead	(siga) derecho	(**see**-gah) deh-**reh**-choh
near	cerca	**sehr**-kah
far	lejos	**leh**-hohs
more	más	mahs
less	menos	**meh**-nohs
entrance	entrada	ehn-**trah**-dah
exit	salida	sah-**lee**-dah
elevator	el ascensor	ehl ah-sehn-**sohr**
toilets	baños	**bah**-nyohs
women's	de damas	deh **dah**-mahs
men's	de caballeros	deh kah-bah-**yeh**-rohs

Post Offices and Banks

Where can I change money?	¿Dónde puedo cambiar dinero?	**dohn**-deh **pweh**-doh kahm-bee-**ahr** dee-**neh**-roh
How much is the postage to…?	¿Cuánto cuesta enviar una carta a…?	**kwahn**-toh **kweh**-stah ehn-vee-**yahr oo**-nah **kahr**-tah ah
I need stamps	Necesito estampillas	neh-seh-**see**-toh ehs-tahm-**pee**-yahs

Shopping

How much does this cost?	¿Cuánto cuesta esto?	**kwahn**-toh **kwehs**-tah **ehs**-toh
I would like…	Me gustaría…	meh goos-tah-**ree**-ah
Do you have?	¿Tienen?	tee-**yeh**-nehn
Do you take credit cards/ traveler's checks?	¿Aceptan tarjetas de crédito/ cheques de viajero?	ah-**sehp**-tahn tahr-**heh**-tahs deh **kreh**-dee-toh/ **cheh**-kehs deh vee-ah-**heh**-roh
I am looking for…	Estoy buscando…	ehs-tohy boos-**kahn**-doh
expensive	caro	**kahr**-oh
cheap	barato	bah-**rah**-toh
white	blanco	**blahn**-koh
black	negro	**neh**-groh
red	rojo	**roh**-hoh
yellow	amarillo	ah-mah-**ree**-yoh
green	verde	**vehr**-deh
blue	azul	ah-**sool**
antique store	la tienda de antigüedades	lah tee-**ehn**-dah deh ahn-tee-gweh-**dah**-dehs
bakery	la panadería	lah pah-nah-deh-**ree**-ah

bank	el banco	ehl **bahn**-koh
bookstore	la librería	lah lee-breh-**ree**-ah
butcher's	la carnicería	lah kahr-nee-seh-**ree**-ah
cake store	la pastelería	lah pahs-teh-leh-**ree**-ah
jeweler's	la joyería	lah hoh-yeh-**ree**-yah
market	el tianguis/mercado	ehl tee-ahn-goo-ees/mehr-**kah**-doh
newsstand	el puesto de periódicos	ehl **puh**-as-toh deh pe-rio-dee-kohs
post office	la oficina de correos	lah oh-fee-**see**-nah deh kohr-**reh**-ohs
shoe store	la zapatería	lah sah-pah-teh-**ree**-ah
supermarket	el supermercado	ehl soo-pehr-mehr-**kah**-doh
travel agency	la agencia de viajes	lah ah-**hehn**-see-ah deh vee-**ah**-hehs

Transportation

When does the... leave?	¿A qué hora sale el...?	ah keh oh-rah sah-leh ehl
Where is the bus stop?	¿Dónde está la parada de buses?	dohn-deh ehs-**tah** lah pah-**rah**-dah deh **boo**-sehs
Is there a bus/train to...?	¿Hay un camión/tren a...?	eye oon kah-mee-**ohn**/trehn ah...?
platform	el andén	ehl ahn-**dehn**
ticket office	la taquilla	lah tah-**kee**-yah
round-trip ticket	un boleto de ida y vuelta	oon boh-**leh**-toh deh ee-dah ee voo-**ehl**-tah
one-way ticket	un boleto de ida solamente	oon boh-**leh**-toh deh ee-dah soh-lah-**mehn**-teh
airport	el aeropuerto	ehl ah-ehr-oh-**poo**-ehr-toh

Sightseeing

art gallery	el museo de arte	ehl moo-**seh**-oh deh **ahr**-teh
beach	la playa	lah **plah**-yah
cathedral	la catedral	lah kah-teh-**drahl**
church	la iglesia/la basílica	lah ee-**gleh**-see-ah/lah bah-**see**-lee-kah
garden	el jardín	ehl hahr-**deen**
museum	el museo	ehl moo-**seh**-oh
pyramid	la pirámide	lah pee-**rah**-meed
ruins	las ruinas	lahs roo-ee-nahs
tourist information office	la oficina de turismo	lah oh-fee-see-nah deh too-**rees**-moh
ticket	la entrada	lah ehn-**trah**-dah
guide (person)	el/la guía	ehl/lah **gee**-ah

guide (book)	la guía	lah **gee**-ah
map	el mapa	ehl **mah**-pah
taxi stand	sitio de taxis	see-tee-oh deh **tahk**-sees

Staying in a Hotel

Do you have a vacant room?	¿Tienen una habitación libre?	tee-eh-nehn oo-nah ah-bee-tah-see-**ohn** lee-breh
double room	habitación doble	ah-bee-tah-see-**ohn** doh-bleh
single room	habitación sencilla	ah-bee-tah-see-**ohn** sehn-**see**-yah
room with a bath	habitación con baño	ah-bee-tah-see-**ohn** kohn **bah**-nyoh
shower	la ducha	lah **doo**-chah
I have a reservation	Tengo una habitación reservada	tehn-goh oo-nah ah-bee-tah-see-**ohn** reh-sehr-**vah**-dah
key	la llave	lah **yah**-veh

Eating Out

Have you got a table for...	¿Tienen mesa para...?	tee-eh-nehn meh-sah pah-**rah**
I want to reserve a table	Quiero reservar una mesa	kee-eh-roh reh-sehr-**vahr** oo-nah meh-sah
The bill, please	La cuenta, por favor	lah kwehn-tah pohr fah-**vohr**
I am a vegetarian	Soy vegetariano/a	soy veh-heh-tah-ree-**ah**-no/na
waiter/waitress	mesero/a	meh-**seh**-roh/rah
menu	la carta	lah **kahr**-tah
wine list	la carta de vinos	lah **kahr**-tah deh **vee**-nohs
glass	un vaso	oon **vah**-soh
bottle	una botella	oo-nah boh-**teh**-yah
knife	un cuchillo	oon koo-**chee**-yoh
fork	un tenedor	oon teh-neh-**dohr**
spoon	una cuchara	oo-nah koo-**chah**-rah
breakfast	el desayuno	ehl deh-sah-**yoo**-noh
lunch	la comida	lah koh-**mee**-dah
dinner	la cena	lah **seh**-nah
main course	el plato fuerte	ehl **plah**-toh foo-**ehr**-teh
starters	las entradas	lahs ehn-**trah**-das
dish of the day	el plato del día	ehl **plah**-toh dehl **dee**-ah
tip	la propina	lah proh-**pee**-nah
Is service included?	¿El servicio está incluido?	ehl sehr-**vee**-see-oh ehs-**tah** een-kloo-ee-doh

Menu Decoder

el aceite	ah-see-eh-teh	oil
las aceitunas	ah-seh-toon-ahs	olives
el agua mineral	ah-gwa mee-neh-rahl	mineral water
sin gas/con gas	seen gas/kohn gas	still/sparkling
el ajo	ah-hoh	garlic
el arroz	ahr-rohs	rice
el azúcar	ah-soo-kahr	sugar
una bebida	beh-bee-dah	drink
el café	kah-feh	coffee
la carne	kahr-neh	meat
la cebolla	seh-boh-yah	onion
el cerdo	sehr-doh	pork
la cerveza	sehr-veh-sah	beer
el chocolate	choh-koh-lah-teh	chocolate
la ensalada	ehn-sah-lah-dah	salad
la fruta	froo-tah	fruit
el helado	eh-lah-doh	ice cream
el huevo	oo-eh-voh	egg
el jugo	hoo-goh	juice
la langosta	lahn-gohs-tah	lobster
la leche	leh-cheh	milk
la mantequilla	mahn-teh-kee-yah	butter
la manzana	mahn-sah-nah	apple
los mariscos	mah-rees-kohs	seafood
la naranja	nah-rahn-hah	orange
el pan	pahn	bread
las papas	pah-pahs	potatoes
el pescado	pehs-kah-doh	fish
picante	pee-kahn-teh	spicy
la pimienta	pee-mee-yehn-tah	pepper
el plátano	pla-tah-noh	banana
el pollo	poh-yoh	chicken
el postre	pohs-treh	dessert
el queso	keh-soh	cheese
el refresco	reh-frehs-koh	soft drink/soda
la sal	sahl	salt
la salsa	sahl-sah	sauce
la sopa	soh-pah	soup
el té	teh	herb tea (usually camomile)
el té negro	teh neh-groh	tea
la torta	tohr-tah	sandwich
las tostadas	tohs-tah-dahs	toast
el vinagre	vee-nah-greh	vinegar
el vino blanco	vee-noh blahn-koh	white wine
el vino tinto	vee-noh teen-toh	red wine

Numbers

0	cero	seh-roh
1	uno	oo-noh
2	dos	dohs
3	tres	trehs
4	cuatro	kwa-troh
5	cinco	seen-koh
6	seis	says
7	siete	see-eh-teh
8	ocho	oh-choh
9	nueve	nweh-veh
10	diez	dee-ehs
11	once	ohn-seh
12	doce	doh-seh
13	trece	treh-seh
14	catorce	kah-tohr-seh
15	quince	keen-seh
16	dieciséis	dee-eh-see-seh-ees
17	diecisiete	dee-eh-see-see-eh-teh
18	dieciocho	dee-eh-see-oh-choh
19	diecinueve	dee-eh-see-nweh-veh
20	veinte	veh-een-teh
21	veintiuno	veh-een-tee-oo-noh
22	veintidós	veh-een-tee-dohs
30	treinta	treh-een-tah
31	treinta y uno	treh-een-tah ee oo-noh
40	cuarenta	kwah-rehn-tah
50	cincuenta	seen-kwehn-tah
60	sesenta	seh-sehn-tah
70	setenta	seh-tehn-tah
80	ochenta	oh-chehn-tah
90	noventa	noh-vehn-tah
100	cien	see-ehn
101	ciento uno	see-ehn-toh oo-noh
102	ciento dos	see-ehn-toh dohs
200	doscientos	dohs-see-ehn-tohs
500	quinientos	khee-nee-ehn-tohs
700	setecientos	seh-teh-see-ehn-tohs
900	novecientos	noh-veh-see-ehn-tohs
1,000	mil	meel
1,001	mil uno	meel oo-noh

Time

one minute	un minuto	oon mee-noo-toh
one hour	una hora	oo-nah oh-rah
half an hour	media hora	meh-dee-ah oh-rah
half past one	la una y media	lah oo-nah ee meh-dee-ah
Monday	lunes	loo-nehs
Tuesday	martes	mahr-tehs
Wednesday	miércoles	mee-ehr-koh-lehs
Thursday	jueves	hoo-eh-vehs
Friday	viernes	vee-ehr-nehs
Saturday	sábado	sah-bah-doh
Sunday	domingo	doh-meen-goh